# The Pleasure Path to Wealth

## How To Get Everything You Want Using The Power Of Your Female Orgasm

Amanda Goldston

## Copyright notice

First published in the UK in 2018 by Amanda Goldston,
29 Victoria Road, Tamworth, Staffordshire, B79 7HU
© 2018 Amanda Goldston
Text copyright © 2018 Amanda Goldston
Compilation copyright © 2018 Amanda Goldston
Illustrations copyright © 2018 Gregory Goldston
Cover design, and other images © 2018 Gregory Goldston
Front and rear cover images © 2018 Andrew Wood Photography

ISBN: 978-1-908253-24-8

A CIP catalogue record for this book is available from the British Library

All rights reserved. No part of this workbook may be reproduced or utilized in any form or by any means, electronic or mechanical, including photocopying, recording or by any information storage and retrieval system, without the prior written permission of the author or the publisher.

Amanda Goldston asserts the moral right to be identified as the author of this work.

Amanda Goldston

http://www.ThePleasurePathToWealth.com

## Disclaimer

The information in "The Pleasure Path to Wealth" book is for information and entertainment purposes only.

The persons who have produced and contributed to this book do not have any medical, scientific, psychological, health (including without limitation mental health), hypnosis, coaching, mediation, therapy, neuro linguistic programming, business, financial qualification or background in any of these areas or similar areas.

Amanda Goldston, her directors, employees and agents make no warranty or representation that they have any specific skills or expertise. No warranty or representation is made that the use of any products will achieve a specific effect, result or purpose.

Amanda Goldston, her officers, employees and agents have no responsibility for any decision or action which you decide to take based on the use of the (including losses, damages, costs and expenses which you or others may incur) based on any information available in this workbook.

You must use you own skill and judgement in deciding whether the "The Pleasure Path to Wealth" is suitable for you. Amanda Goldston, her officers, employees and agents make no recommendations, warranties or representations about the suitability of the book for any person.

We recommend that if there are any health (mental, physical or otherwise), medical, business, financial or any other issues which are or may be affecting your life or upon which you need advice, you should obtain advice from an appropriate qualified professional person.

*Contents*

| | |
|---|---|
| INTRODUCTION | 11 |
| CHAPTER ONE – WHAT IS ORGASM ENERGY? | 13 |
| CHAPTER TWO – THE CLITORIS AND YOUR PLEASURE | 22 |
| CHAPTER THREE – WAYS TO STIMULATE ORGASM ENERGY | 35 |
| CHAPTER FOUR – HOW TO POWER UP YOUR ORGASM ENERGY | 49 |
| CHAPTER FIVE – HOW TO USE ORGASM ENERGY FOR INCREASED PROSPERITY | 57 |
| CHAPTER SIX – ORGASMIC GOALS AND INTENTIONS | 72 |
| CHAPTER SEVEN – OTHER BENEFITS TO USING YOUR ORGASM ENERGY | 76 |
| CHAPTER EIGHT – POSITIVE CHANGES IN YOU AS A PERSON | 85 |
| CHAPTER NINE – SEXUAL HEALING | 89 |
| CHAPTER TEN – THE DOWNSIDES AND WARNINGS! | 97 |
| CHAPTER ELEVEN IT'S ALL CONNECTED! HOORAY! | 114 |

CHAPTER TWELVE – PLEASURE RULES OK! ................................................................. 125

ABOUT THE AUTHOR – AMANDA GOLDSTON ......................................................... 129

OTHER RESOURCES ........................................ 133

CONTACT .......................................................... 135

## Preface

This book is about the pleasure that comes from the female orgasm and how that power can be harnessed to create prosperity in life and business.

This book is based on my personal experiences and research which I have carried out on this subject.

It is partly the story of my own journey and how I came to discover this wonderful material and partly practical tips that YOU can use to tap into the power of your own Orgasm Energy and create miracles in your life.

Please use this book as a springboard for further exploration.

## Sex Education 101!

I attended an all girls' convent school in the late 1970s/early 1980s. I remember one day, when I was around 15 and it was a Biology lesson. I walked into the classroom and the old nun, who was the Biology Teacher, was standing at the front of the blank blackboard, with her arms folded. She informed us that today's lesson was on human reproduction. She went on to tell us that there was a lot of smut around that subject.

She then pulled down the rolling board, which had pictures of the female reproduction system and the male reproductive system. We were instructed to copy them down as fast as possible, as they would not be staying on the board after the lesson.

That was it! Sex Education 101! The subject was not mentioned again in any other lesson!

I have come a long way from there!

## My Inspiration

One of my biggest sources of inspiration has been Napoleon Hill and his book, "*Think and Grow Rich*", which was first published in 1935. In it, he talked about The Tenth Step towards Riches as "The Mystery of Sex: Transmutation."

Napoleon Hill links love, sex and romance with money and business success, although the actual steps on how to connect and use these things are unclear.

This concept is probably the least understood, certainly the least talked about, however I believe this is one of the most important Principles of Success.

I first read this book in my early twenties and although I had not consciously used this material, I had subconsciously acted upon it to create personal and business success. It was only during the course of 2014 that I finally came to understand this principle as I saw it unfold in my own life.

I have now updated that principle to make it workable for the 21$^{st}$ century woman to bring increased prosperity and success in your business.

## INTRODUCTION

**Once upon a time** there was a woman who wanted an easier way to create money and success in her life than the way she was currently doing things.

**Every day** she went to a job that she disliked, where she worked long hours to make money. At the end of the day she felt totally drained, with no energy for anything else in her life.

**One day** she was introduced to the gift of receiving pleasure in her body from her own female orgasm.

**Because of that** she glowed with radiant, sensual, female energy and became almost magnetic to people, opportunities and success.

**Because of that** her income increased so she worked less hours, which meant she had less stress and more time for herself and her family.

**Until finally** she put herself and her pleasure as her number one priority, which meant she made different choices. This enabled her to courageously and confidently create a new career for herself doing what she loved - teaching other women about the power of their pleasure and their orgasmic energies for increased wealth, health and happiness.

## Orgasm and Pleasure Leads to Prosperity Beyond Measure!

When you make YOU and YOUR PLEASURE as your NUMBER ONE PRIORITY, then everything flows.

YOU are the Source of your PLEASURE and your ORGASMS in your body.

### Treat Yourself Like a Queen and Expect to Receive Pleasure

When you feel good about yourself, it becomes a self-perpetuating cycle. Treat yourself like the Queen that you are, use words like 1$^{st}$ class, opulent and luxurious when you talk about yourself and your life. Ask for what you truly want and expect to receive it in ways that is most pleasurable to you.

# CHAPTER ONE – WHAT IS ORGASM ENERGY?

## Orgasm is Pleasure!

## What is Orgasm Energy?

This is probably a good place to talk about what exactly is Orgasm energy and perhaps, equally important, what it is not, so we are on the same page.

## Climax Experience

According to the Oxford English Dictionary the definition of an orgasm is "*The climax of sexual excitement, characterised by intensely pleasurable feelings, centred in the genitals and (in men) experienced as an accompaniment to ejaculation.*"

The origins of the word Orgasm are from the late seventeenth century French "Orgasme," or from the modern Latin "Orgasmus" and from the Greek, "Orgasmos" meaning "Organ Swell or Be Excited." Interestingly, all of these words are masculine in origin!

## A Climax is Not Necessarily the Same as an Orgasm

All the definitions are focused around the male orgasm, which more often than not happens at the same time as a climax and ejaculation. It is possible for a man to have the sensations of an orgasm and not climax, although that can lead to a lot of frustration.

A woman can quite easily experience an orgasm or multiple orgasms and not actually climax.

A climax is considered to be a build-up of energy that generally happens during sexual intercourse to a point where it sort of "tips over the edge" or "explodes" in your body, which leads to a huge release of energy.

**The Origin of an Orgasm**

People often think of an orgasm as being located in the sexual areas of the body. This is partly true. There is great debate as to the exact origin of an orgasm for a woman, whether it is within the vagina or whether it comes from the clitoris or whether it is a combination of both.

Women often say that they have never experienced an orgasm. This is usually when they are defining their orgasm as a climax at the end of sexual intercourse, whether that is with a partner or from their own masturbation. This usually relates to the vagina being penetrated by the penis or a sexual toy.

More recent studies have shown that it is actually the clitoris, and not the vagina, that is the source of most orgasms.

**Female Orgasm**

Orgasms can be happening on a continuous basis in your body. An Orgasm is a major contributor to your life-force energy. Orgasm energy is the feelings and sensations that run around the whole body, not just in the sexual areas and genitals. They can be anything from a little ripple that almost feels like a shiver or a tickle, to a full blown shaking of your body – and pretty much anything in between!

An Orgasm produces energy which feels amazing and buzzes and tingles through your entire body. It is a continuous revving of little electrical pulses that are flowing around your body.

The female orgasm is a sensual energy, which intensifies all the senses of the body. This includes the usual five senses of sight, sound, touch, smell and taste and also the inner sixth sense of intuition. This is a huge benefit for anyone in business.

**Orgasms Everywhere**

An orgasm can take place anywhere in your body where the muscles are contracting and relaxing, so if you feel tingles in your feet, you might well be having a foot-gasm, or you feel prickles of excitement running up your arm, that could be an arm-gasm and if you feel your heart suddenly open wide with love, then that could be a heart –gasm. You might even feel your whole body expanding and contracting and yes, that is appropriately called a whole body orgasm.

Orgasm does not have to happen purely on the back of sexual activity. Nor is it limited to self-pleasuring, although that can be a good way to stimulate it initially. This is particularly good news for those who are currently single! Orgasms can also happen from other activities such as laughing, dancing and deep breathing.

Having said that, one of the quickest and easiest ways to stimulate an orgasm is through touching and stroking the clitoris.

The Clitoris is designed solely for your pleasure and she quickly responds to any attention.

Once you know what Orgasm energy feels like, then with practice, you can re-create those feelings, just by remembering them in your body and intensifying them. You can flow the energy around your body to give your whole body pleasure. Yes, you can experience an orgasm just by sitting still and feeling immensely good.

**Notice the Feelings in Your Body**

Take the time to really connect with yourself and your body and the feelings and sensations that are going on in her. Observe if you have tingles in your feet or perhaps you feel some part of your body is throbbing or pulsating with energy. That might well be little mini orgasms happening in your body and this can be your body telling you she is happy.

The more familiar you are with your own body, the more you can appreciate the pleasure that she wants to give you.

**Signs of Orgasm**

There are some simple signs that your body is going into orgasm. The lips of your labia around your vagina will often go a deep pink or crimson colour and everything swells up. There is likely to be considerable wetness around your genitals. Orgasm is often characterised by rapid contractions around the whole area, including the perineum, which is located between the opening of the vagina and the anus. The anus itself can start to contract. It is likely that your vaginal muscles will begin to contract, giving sensations of pleasure.

After an orgasm, it is likely that your breasts will be swollen and your nipples may be erect. They may be little flushes of red on your chest. It is likely that your face has some red colouring especially around your ears.

Look in the mirror after an orgasm and you will see that your skin looks younger. This is because your skin has just had an influx of nourishing blood. My husband has often said I look 20 years younger after an orgasm – I certainly feel it.

Interestingly, you may get comments on how lovely your make-up looks, even though you might not be wearing any. All you have done is have Orgasms. Make-up was actually invented to replicate the signs of Orgasm, which are full lips, dilated pupils in the eyes and flushed cheeks!

**Trigger Spot**

You can train any part of your body to be a trigger spot for your orgasm and it does not have to be in your genital area. It could be in your little finger, your elbow or any place on your body.

When you touch that spot in some way, it triggers off all the feelings of orgasmic energy, which start flowing around your body and you feel really good.

It has been said that baby girls can trigger an orgasm in their bodies, just by rubbing the tops of their legs together. They have never been trained how to do this. They just know instinctively that it is something that gives them pleasure and probably leads to an eruption of giggling and a big smile!

There is a spot in your mouth called the Palate, which is at the roof of your mouth. This is a very sensitive area and is often thought of as one of the gateways or triggers to higher intelligence and to pleasure. Try putting the tip of your tongue on this area as you breathe deeply and send energy around your body.

The palm of the hand can be very sensitive to gentle touch!

## The Hormones of Orgasm

There are two very important hormones released during Orgasm, which are Serotonin and Oxytocin. Serotonin is known as the Happy Hormone and Oxytocin is the Love and Connection Hormone.

## The Release of Serotonin – Happy Hormones!

Serotonin is known as the Happy Hormone. It creates feelings of happiness, joy and general well-being. An absence of Serotonin is considered to be one of the primary causes of depression, and Serotonin forms the basis of many anti-depressant medication products.

Serotonin is found in two places in the body. One is in the pleasure centres in the brain, however the majority, between 80 and 90%, is located in the digestive tract or the gut. Orgasms release serotonin, which floods your body and brain with powerful happy hormones.

As most serotonin is released into your body from your digestive tract, this means that you are likely to feel physically better in your body first. This is almost instantaneously followed by the serotonin being triggered in your brain, which leads to your mood improving and your emotions feeling lighter.

In this place, you are likely to adopt a more optimistic outlook on life, which means that you can be more open to finding solutions to problems. You start to look for possibilities and ways to move forward, rather than getting stuck in challenges. Your mantra becomes "How could I do that?" rather than "I can't."

All this inevitably causes you to feel much better about yourself, which can trigger the start of an upward spiral of positivity and pleasure.

**The Release of Oxytocin for Love and Connection**

The other hormone that is released during Orgasm is Oxytocin, which is affectionately known as the Love and Connection Hormone. It is released by mothers when they are breast-feeding babies to create a bond and a connection.

It is the hormone that causes you to want to connect with other people and to have a meaningful relationship with them. It is what enables women to really flourish in communities of other women, where everyone can feel nourished and supported.

The hormone often drives men insane because we ask them constantly, "Yes, I know that is what happened, but how do you FEEL about that?" It is not that men don't feel, they just have a different way of expressing their feelings.

Oxytocin can lead to a desire for collaboration and to creating situations where everyone wins. When this feeds into the Upward Spiral of Positivity, it becomes hugely powerful.

Interestingly the more you allow yourself to experience pleasure, and make pleasure your top priority, the more you value yourself and the more likely you are to look for partnerships where you gain as much as everyone else.

This creates a big dose of ME TOO instead of Me Last! You may even find that you experience feelings of "ME FIRST!" This is an interesting place to be for women, as it directly contradicts the programming that most of us have received all of our lives, that we have to put everyone else first and ourselves last.

When that belief system comes to the surface, it is important to really look closely at it and see how much – if any – is actually relevant to you today.

As you start to work with your own Pleasure and putting yourself first, you may find you hear words such as "Selfish Bitch" being thrown at you. Be ready for them, as they are signs that other people can no longer control and manipulate you and that you are putting your needs first. Regular Orgasms can also be the antidote that helps to clear those old patterns.

Orgasms and Pleasure are game changers. They alter the state of your mind, body and emotions for the better. The ripple effect throughout your whole life can be enormous and almost immeasurable.

## CHAPTER TWO – THE CLITORIS AND YOUR PLEASURE

### The Clitoris

The clitoris is an organ in your body that is dedicated solely to your pleasure. It has no other function in your body. As such it is worthy of a whole chapter to itself.

Studies have shown that the clitoris is actually a lot more extensive than anyone had previously thought. It is only since 1998 that we have had a true picture of the scope and size of the clitoris. This was thanks to the pioneering work of Dr Helen O'Connell, who used MRI Scanning to give us 3D pictures of the clitoris.

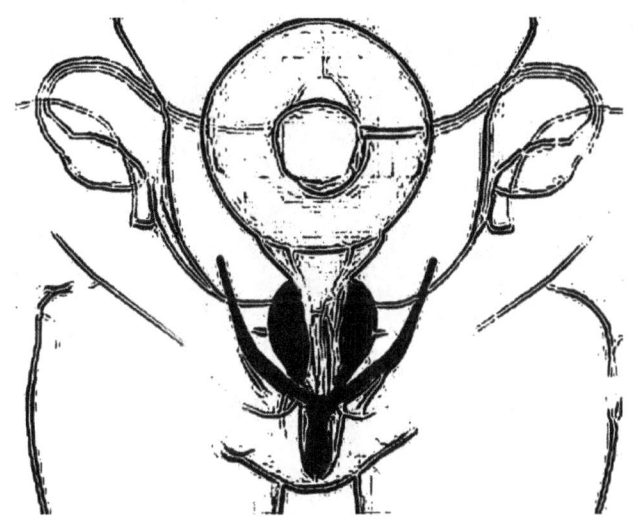

As you can see from the diagram, the clitoris extends down behind your vagina and wraps around it at the base, almost giving it a hug. Your clitoris is almost 9cm /4" in length- and that is before it is stimulated. The clitoris has the little wings, which point upwards towards your back, when aroused. It swells around the vagina area, which means that if you are also having sexual intercourse, then the vagina is going to be much tighter. For a man inserting his penis (or his lingam – wand of light- as the Eastern Traditions call it) – then he is going to be getting more sensation and pleasure, as well as enhancing your own pleasure.

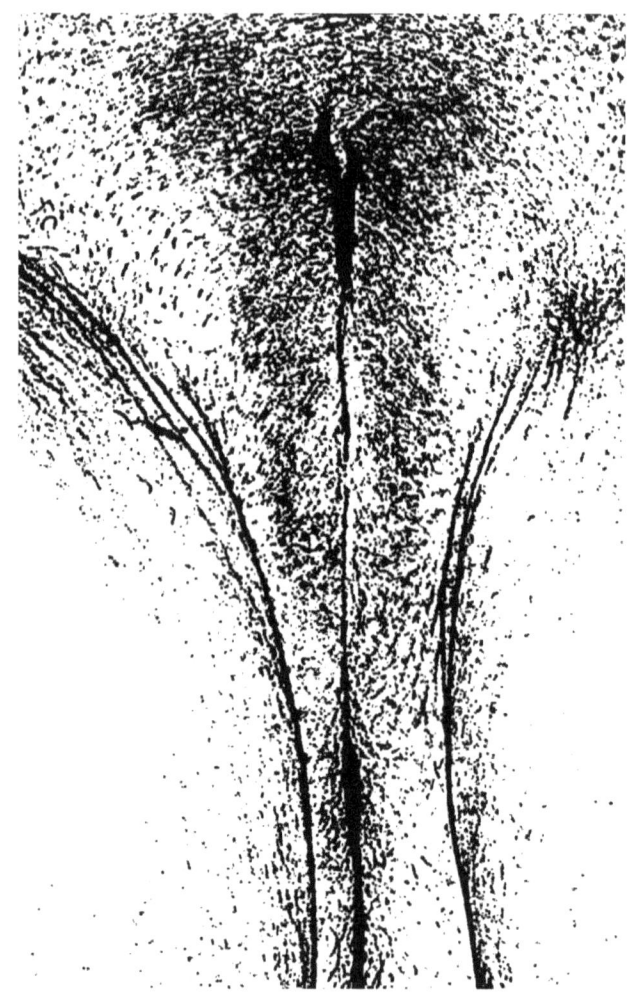

This is a drawing of a Vagina and clitoris that is asleep

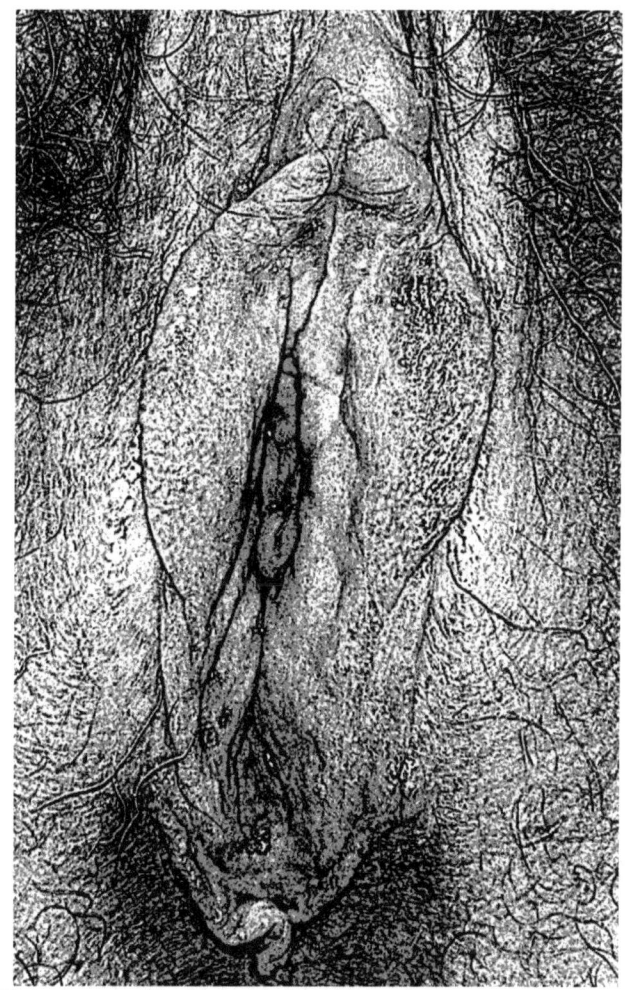
This shows a Vagina and clitoris that has been stroked and stimulated.

You can see from the drawings the huge physical difference that takes place between a clitoris that is unstimulated and one which has been stroked and pleasured to orgasm. You can how the vagina has swollen as well, and that is without any penetration.

This means that pleasure can actually be felt right through your whole pelvic area. There are over 8000 nerve endings on the head of the clitoris alone, which is more than twice the number found on a male penis. These clitoris nerve endings connect with numerous parts of the female brain, including pleasure centres. This means that the pleasure created by an orgasm can ripple through your whole body, leaving you feeling amazing.

This is very important when we think of our upward spiral of positivity. Introduce Pleasure in the form of an Orgasm and watch your positive spiral soar upwards.

**Stroking the Clitoris**

The Clitoris is the powerhouse of your pleasure. Generally she likes to be stroked quite gently, in order to be stimulated to pleasure. She does not appreciate rough treatment and only accepts vigorous rubbing when she is in the mood for that. If she is not in the mood, she will just withdraw under her little hood and hide. Yes, it is quite fair to say, she does have a mind of her own!

For a lot of sexual activity, a woman generally needs to be "in the mood" emotionally to get anything from it. With stroking the clitoris, it does not really matter what mood you are in. You can simply lie back and focus on the pleasure sensations in your body. It also does not matter whether you "climax" or not. In fact you can have multiple orgasms of tingling, rippling sensations in your body, without actually having a "climax."

Sometimes, for me, if my body does not wish to give me a climax, some of the most intense orgasm sensations are on the bottoms of my feet or behind my ears!

**Pleasure Points**

The head of the clitoris itself has multiple pleasure points on it. In fact the whole thing is one big sensitive, pleasure point. It is just a matter of finding exactly where on your clitoris gives you personally the most pleasure.

When gently stroked, the whole area from the pubic bone right down and round to the anus can give pleasure.

Yes, the G-spot does exist and can be a source of huge enjoyment, especially when touched in combination with stroking the clitoris. It is located inside the vagina, almost directly behind the clitoris.

Finding your personal pleasure points is a journey of exploration, which you might want to do on your own or with a partner.

In my opinion it is a very good idea to explore your own clitoris.

Get yourself a mirror and have a good look at her and your whole genital area. Look at her shape, her colours and discover how she likes to be touched. Notice what responses you get and how much pleasure she can give you in your body, when you allow her to do that for you. Perhaps give her a name – and make it something kind, loving and complimentary!

When you know exactly how you like to be touched, you can then share that information with a partner, if you wish, so that they know exactly what to do to bring you the most pleasure.

The clitoris is quite often referred to as a "pussy" which I think is a lovely term to describe the whole area.

It certainly has the same reaction when stroked as you would get from stroking a real feline. It can cause you to purr like a contented pussy cat, especially after a gorgeous orgasm.

It is the seat of your personal power as a woman and is what can cause you to become a Roaring Lioness when need be!

## Orgasmic Pleasuring – Partnered Process

Making time for touch, orgasm and sensual pleasure can have a profoundly positive effect on your personal relationships.

Let me tell you a little bit about OP-ing or Orgasmic Pleasuring. This is a partnered process, whereby you, as the woman, lie back with your legs butterflied open and you have your clitoris gently stroked for anywhere from 10 -20 minutes.

The person who is doing the stroking, who can be male or female, remains fully clothed. This is a practice that has no goals, other than for you to feel pleasure. There is no expectation for you to do anything in return for your pleasure giver. It might be a foreplay to sex or it can be an entirely self-contained process. It depends on you and your partner, how you feel after an OP-ing session and what time you have got.

## Men Want to Make Women Happy

What I have discovered is that most men what to make us women happy and to give us pleasure. Yes, they do! Really! That is often one of their primary driving forces. The trouble is that most of them don't know how to make a woman happy, because we ourselves, as women, don't really know what would make us happy!

This is one of the joys of OP-ing. It is a very simple practice, where you can give your partner (male or female) quite clear instructions as to what to do and where to touch you, in order to create the maximum amount of pleasure.

Men, in particular, respond really well to this because it gives them the opportunity to provide you with exactly what you desire. It takes away the pressure of them trying to figure out what they need to do.

**What Do Men Get Out of OP-ing?**

So, what do men get out of OP-ing? Quite a lot actually. Men love to look at and admire women's bodies. If you are in a relationship, your partner is likely to welcome the opportunity to really examine and caress your body. For some women, this can be the first time they have allowed their partners to do that.

One of the things is that they get to look at and stroke your pussy for 10-20 minutes, or longer if you so desire. This gives men huge amounts of pleasure, as they are often not really given the opportunity to do that. In giving you pleasure, this makes many men very happy.

OP-ing is a process that cannot be done under the sheets with the lights out.

OP-ing hugely increases intimacy and connection. Although there are often few words actually spoken, you, as the receiver have the opportunity to ask for exactly what you want, even if that is just a lighter pressure with a stroke.

It can be quite a vulnerable place and it is important that you feel safe and respected.

As you are now experiencing more orgasms and pleasure in your life, it is very likely that your overall sexual appetite will increase. It might not happen straight off the back of an OP-ing session, nor should it be expected, but it is very likely that you, as a woman, will be highly turned on and thus desiring more "regular sex" in your life. So men give the gift of OP-ing and get more attention and more sex back in return.

### Personal Pleasuring – Just You

You are the source of your own pleasure. You don't need anyone else to create pleasure for you in your body. You might choose to massage and stroke yourself and you might choose to use sex toys that are readily available.

If you use sex toys, make sure you follow the instructions for use, as well as keeping them clean.

## Touch

This is probably one of the biggest ways of creating orgasm energy in your body. There are different levels of touch, ranging from very soft and gentle, where you are barely touching the skin to quite vigorous rubbing.

Touch is one of the most fundamental human requirements for survival, especially when it is done in a loving way.

Give yourself the gift of touch – perhaps when you come out of the bath or shower and your skin already feels soft. Take the time to explore your body. Touch it in different ways and see what feels good. As you do this, you can make sounds such as mmm.

Try this now. Touch your arm, stroke it gently and say, "I love you, you are so beautiful, mmm that is gorgeous. This is totally delicious and delectable and I feel sensual, sensuous and beautiful."

Coconut Oil is fabulous for this!

Find out what tickles you, what stimulates you, what makes you laugh and what makes you feel good.

Touch can be something that you do for yourself or it can be something that you do with a partner.

### Say Nice Things To and About Yourself

Telling yourself kind things is extremely important. Your body is unlikely to return you pleasure if you tell her that she is ugly, you hate her or you think she is fat. Find things about yourself that you genuinely appreciate and speak them out loud. Your body hears everything you say to and about her and she responds accordingly. She has no capacity to discern what you say as a joke or in sarcasm. She takes everything literally. Treat her like you would your best friend or the person that you most love in the world.

### Talk Nicely to your Clitoris and Pussy

She is your friend. She is the seat of your feminine power, wisdom, intuition and decision making. Look at her in the mirror, examine her, marvel at her beauty, give her a complimentary name. Ask her to give you all the pleasure she can – she will happily oblige!

## Cliteracy

There is a fascinating exhibition called Cliteracy by Artist Sophia Watson, which gives a lot of information about the clitoris. Sophia has created a banner that is 10 feet by 13 feet with a 6 foot neon sign above it, with the word Cliteracy on it. The banner contains 100 Natural Laws about the Clitoris and Female Sexuality.

One of my favourite quotes from it is, "Democracy without Cliteracy is a Phalluscy."

You can find about the Cliteracy Project from Sophia Wallace's Website, which is http://www.sophiawallace.com/

## CHAPTER THREE – WAYS TO STIMULATE ORGASM ENERGY

There are many different ways that you can create orgasm energy in your body. The point of this is that whatever you do creates a feeling of immense pleasure for you. Choose what works for you.

It is very easy to tap into these energies and to harness them at will. Once you know what orgasm energy feels like to you personally, you can then trigger it easily in a variety of ways. This may or may not involve sex and it may or not involve another person.

Most of these techniques can be quick, short and done in a matter of minutes at various points throughout the day. You do not need any lengthy routines or special equipment. I have found that I have made more time for my pleasure in my day, so I often combine several of these together to make a longer pleasuring experience for myself.

### Upward Spiral of Positivity

All of these techniques are designed so that you can inject pleasure into your life and project yourself in an upwards direction on the positive spiral.

### Re-Create the Orgasm State

If you know you have previously experienced an orgasm, it is possible to put yourself back in that space and allow those feelings to bubble up in your body.

You can recreate that feeling in a number of ways, which might be simply recalling an incident where you had an orgasm or even gently stroking your orgasm trigger point.

I was at an event recently, where I told a lady that you cannot have the pleasurable feelings of orgasm in your body at the same time as the negative feelings of unworthiness or not good enough. It is one or the other. The lady disagreed, stating that she had experienced both feelings at the same time. She then proceeded to tell me her story, where she had been in a business meeting and suddenly felt her knickers get very wet and tingling sensations in her clitoris area.

Yes, her she-body, with a wicked sense of humour, had decided it was high time to lighten things up a bit and to give her an orgasm at that precise moment!

In just telling me about that incident, the lady re-experienced those same orgasm feelings in her body.

The reason she had disagreed with me was that she had felt guilt and shame arise very quickly, as soon as she started to experience her orgasm energy. Actually she did not experience them both together but one triggered the other. She recognised this to be an old pattern from childhood and we were able to clear it in that moment.

Your body can only experience things in this moment. It cannot tell the difference between a past, present or future event. All it knows is that you are talking about it, so it creates those feelings for you NOW!

This could be a tingling in your body or a feeling of little contractions. This might be in your genitals or it might not. You might also find yourself wriggling about, especially if you are feeling sensations in your sexual area. You may notice other physical signs, such as your face flushing, your nipples enlarging and a feeling of wetness in your knickers or panties.

### How to Think Yourself into Orgasm

Yes, this really can happen.

Sit quietly with your eyes closed, breathe deeply and command your body to go into a state of orgasm – and it will – as long as you expect it to do that.

Let those feelings ripple through your body. If they are located in a certain area, then flow those feelings all round your body.

## Meditation

Yes, it is possible to have an orgasm whilst in meditation, and it is the weirdest feeling!

From my experience, pleasure sensations in the body can override the chatter going on in the mind. Breathe deeply and focus on the word ORGASM. Keep repeating that word, either silently or out loud and let your body create those sensations for you. It does not take long.

## Love and Orgasm Breathing

Breathe deeply and rhythmically, deep in your belly or abdomen area. Become aware of your energy and thoughts whizzing round in your head, then imagine a tube or maybe an escalator or some way of being able to drop that energy from your head down into your body. Feel it pass through the heart area, which might be your physical heart or your spiritual heart centre, which is located in the centre of your chest.

As the energy passes through this area, feel it gathering love, which is then being spread throughout your body. Drop your energy down into the area where your womb is (or would be), feel your energy filling this whole area and breathe deeply.

Remember, this is the seat of your power, and where manifesting and creating happens. If you have any issues where you would like honest, accurate and clear answers, this is the place to ask for that wisdom and guidance.

### Flowing Energy Around Your Body

Orgasm energy is those little ripples of pleasurable sensations that occur anywhere in your body. When you notice them and can feel them, you can then flow that energy around your body. This is done by using the energy lines that run all around your body.

You can also do this by just focusing on any part of your body and really noticing what sensations are there. For example you could focus on your hand and see if you can feel any little movement under your skin. You can also gently stroke your hand and notice what sensations there are in your hand. The sensations might even start to move up your arm.

### Feel Good

Remember a time when you felt really good about yourself and notice how that intensifies the energy feelings in your body.

### Inner Smile

Be kind to yourself. Imagine an inner smile, which is a big, bright ray of happy sunshine that is filling your body, from the top of your head to the tip of your toes. Remember when you felt warm and cosy and snug, with a big smile on your face. Then make that memory bigger and brighter. Remember how good you felt and keep increasing that feeling of well-being. Imagine that smile reaching every part of your body and giving it a kind, gentle, loving hug.

## Sounds of Creation - AA, OO, MM, AUM, OM

Sounds are very important. There are certain sounds which are considered to be fundamental to the whole creation process.

These are AA, OO and MM and when combined form the sound of AUM or OM, which is often considered to be the sound of God, the Universe or Creation.

If you allow them to, these are the sounds that tend to naturally form during sex and particularly during an orgasmic experience. And, Yes, it is a very good idea to let them out!

## AH Meditation – Dr Pillai

There is a wonderful meditation that you can do to harness the power of the sound AH to manifest what you desire in your life. It comes from Dr Pillai of www.pillaicenter.com

This involves using the sound AH to raise the joyful energy that is located in your womb area, or sacreal chakra, up through your spinal column into your brain. Once there you focus on a goal you would like to achieve and fill it with the sound AH to turn it from an idea into physical form.

This is a link to a youtube video with Dr Pillai guiding you through the AH Meditation - https://www.youtube.com/watch?v=j7SaisE81TI

**Singing**

Singing is another fabulous way to get the juices going. Find a song you really love and which uplifts you. Choose a song where you know the words and you can sing along at the top of your voice. If you can combine singing with movement and dance, then so much the better, as you will get double benefit from that. Throw yourself into the song and the music and really take some deep breaths as you do it.

I grew up in the South West of England. In the 1970s, there was a pop group named The Wurzels, which I loved. One of my favourite songs is called "I am a cider drinker." The chorus has sounds that are music to my ears. These are deep throaty, OOOOOOOOOOOAAAAAAAAAAAAWWWWW WWRRRRR, OOOAARR OOAARRWWAA – love it!

## Laughter

Laughter has got to be one of the most powerful things for creating orgasmic energies in your body. When you have a really good belly laugh, so much so that your sides hurt and you might even have tears streaming down your face, then it releases the same endorphins and hormones as a fantastic toe-curling orgasm.

Laughter is a stress reliever and has been shown to be one of the greatest healers in medicine.

Laughter is also contagious and once one person starts laughing, other people will join in, even if they have no idea what anyone else is laughing about.

Laughter forces you to take deep breaths, and is a great releaser of sounds, which is another great way to tap into Orgasm energy.

When laughing uncontrollably, many people tend to pull the strangest of faces, however there are rarely any inhibitions. Most people are more concerned with having a good time, unless, of course, your make-up starts to run, in which case that can cause even more laughter.

## Raucous Cackle

With laughter, I have discovered my Raucous Cackle. I believe every woman should have it in her pleasure box. This is the kind of pixie type giggle, when you have just said "rude" or "naughty" words and you have been told by "serious, responsible adults" that you should not say them, but you like the sound of them, so you are going to say them anyway, like orgasm and sex and pleasure and fun.

Interestingly, a lot of women want to laugh uncontrollable at the end of sex, particularly when they have had a really good orgasm.

A major giggling fit during sex can cause uncontrollable contractions within the vagina.

### Movement and Dance

Movement and dance are great ways to really connect with your body. Pick music that you can really jig along to and that makes you feel really good. You might prefer more sensual type of dancing, where the movement is much slower and you are also touching and stroking your body as you dance.

This can have a more sensual and seductive feel to it. Find something you really enjoy where you can appreciate your body and its movements. Allow yourself to feel really feminine and really in your body. With this type of dancing, you can get yourself very turned on.

Women's bodies are designed to move. We are not designed to be sitting down all day. You might also like to try some dancing and then sit down to meditate. Your meditation can then be extremely empowering and energising.

**Exercise, Especially Pelvic Tilts and Twists**

One useful exercise to do is a Pelvic Tilt. This is where you lie on your back and bend your knees. Lift your knees off the floor and keep your feet flat on the floor. Lift your bottom off the floor and as you do so, squeeze all the muscles in your abdomen and then release them. This is an exercise that is often given to women after childbirth. As you release, feel your whole vagina area opening up. This is a good practice for "Opening to Receive."

As a variation of this, lie on your back, put your feet flat on the floor and raise your knees. Instead of lifting your bottom off the ground, you let your legs drop over to one side or the other, so your knees are pointing one way and you are looking the other way. Move your knees from side to side. This is not a good exercise if you are pregnant because it is a twisting exercise and can potentially cause damage.

Do seek advice from a qualified person before you attempt any exercises.

These are also very effective if you let out a sound such as MMMM or AAAAAA as you breathe out.

## Muscle Tightening

Another way to stimulate orgasm energy is to tighten up your muscles in your vagina area and then release them. As you do so, let out a sound such as aaa or ooo or mmm. These are three of my favourite sounds. They all roll off the tongue in a very sensual, pleasure giving way.

As you relax, feel your vagina relaxing and let your legs fall open – especially if you are lying on your back when you do this.

## Rock on your tailbone (coccyx)

Lie on your back with your knees bent and rock backwards and forwards on your tailbone or coccyx. This is the little bit of bone right at the bottom of your spine, just above the cheeks of your bottom. This is a great way to stimulate an orgasm as it sends energy straight up your spine to the pleasure sensors in your brain.

You can also roll around in a circle, with your tailbone on the floor. This is another great way to stimulate orgasm. You can use the AA, OO and MM sounds to add to your pleasure.

Take your time with it and circle your body and hips in a big circle. This can be intensely pleasurable.

## Massage

This is usually done by someone else for you and can be really beautiful. You can have any part of your body massaged and it may be sexual or it may not. It does not really matter. It is pure, self-indulgent pleasure that leaves you feeling really good. It may be a massage to release and heal a particular issue or it may simply be the joy of being touched and stroked by another human being.

## Yoni Massage

The Yoni is an Eastern term that refers to the whole of the genitals of a woman. It includes the womb, the vaginal canal, the clitoris and the anus. The Yoni massage is done for you by another person and can include any and/or all of these areas, depending on what you want to happen. This is something that you can do yourself to some extent, although it is usually better if you have someone do it for you.

A Yoni Massage can create very intense, multiple orgasms because every sensitive part of your genitals is massaged.

It does not have to be a pre-cursor to sexual intercourse. That depends on the level of trust you have with the person doing the massage for you, your relationship with that person and what you want from them.

Set your own boundaries before you start any of these activities, especially things that might be a bit intimate.

Know what you want and don't want and stick to those boundaries. Be clear with that upfront before you start and don't put yourself in any danger or in situations where you feel uncomfortable.

**Orgasmic Pleasuring**

This is a fantastic way of creating orgasm and pleasure. Please refer back to the previous chapter for a more detailed explanation. It is especially powerful if you can start your day with an OP session because then you go out into the world high on a pleasure cloud. All your positive sensors are firing and you are ready to magnetize magnificent people, opportunities and money

**Joyful Love Making**

This is part of what Napoleon Hill was talking about in his book "*Think and Grow Rich*". Joyful lovemaking, which combines the energy of sex, the emotion of love and maybe a bit of good, old-fashioned romance is a wonderful tonic. Not only does it burn off calories, it brings pleasure and can lead to the triggering of orgasmic energies flowing around your body. This is especially the case if the clitoris has been stimulated first, which heightens the pleasure in your whole pelvic area.

If you breathe deeply while making love, you can increase the sensations of orgasm that are flowing around your body.

Allow yourself to really sink into the moment and experience total physical pleasure. If thoughts come into your mind, then allow those to be gratitude for the gifts of passion and fun that you are receiving.

Before you start your love-making, think of a project you are working on or something where you would like some creative answers. Set an intention that the combination of relaxation, good feelings and energy release gives you the solutions that you are seeking.

I think this is what Napoleon Hill meant by using the transmutation of the sex energy to tap into your genius mind to bring you riches.

When you have finished your love making and you are perhaps lying or sitting quietly, notice what ideas and insights pop into your mind. Then, as soon as you can, act on them! They have come from a very special and powerful place!

I have found it very useful to have a notebook and pen beside my bed to capture these ideas before I forget them.

## CHAPTER FOUR – HOW TO POWER UP YOUR ORGASM ENERGY

### My Daily Rituals

I have put together some rituals for myself to use at different times during the day. You don't have to do all of the steps. You can make the rituals shorter, depending on which ones you personally prefer and also on how much time you have.

### Morning

Getting my Orgasm and Pleasure energy flowing starts as soon as I wake up in the morning.

### Step 1 – Before I get up

a) Before I get up I lie in bed and set my Intention for the day. An example might be "Today I intend to be strong, confident and powerful" or "Today I intend to easily finish my project and it be a joyful experience to do."

b) I think of a goal I want to achieve, SEE myself achieving it, HEAR the words I am saying to myself (or other people are saying to me) as it is accomplished, notice how good I FEEL about accomplishing it and get a sense of what it is like to BE the person who has already accomplished this goal.

c) I breathe deeply and feel the energy flowing down into my body from the Universe and out of my feet into the Earth, so I feel myself to be rooted and grounded into the Earth. I then breathe the energy back up through my body and out the top of my head, so I am connected to my intuition and the wisdom of the Universe.

d) I then imagine the creative energy in my womb area flowing upwards with the sound AH into my brain and then rock backwards and forwards on my tailbone (or coccyx) at the base of my spine, as that can stimulate a little, mini orgasm.

e) I usually take a few more minutes to ask myself "What does the future I desire to create require of me today?" and "What are the 3 most important things I must do today to draw in my goal?" I breathe into my belly and listen to my body for the answers.

I am then ready for my first cup of tea of the day.

## Step 2 – Good Morning Gorgeous

I look in the mirror and say, "Good Morning Gorgeous!" and smile my biggest smile. I then say "I wonder what amazing things are going to happen to me today?" so I set up the expectation of a wonderful day.

## Step 3 – A bit of Stretching

I then stand up straight, breathe deeply and do some simple stretches. I clasp my hands over my head and stretch upwards, then bend backwards and then forwards. I stretch my left arm down my left side and then my right arm down the right side.

I do some hip circles and then move my hips from side to side. This is a good exercise for women to do as it frees up stuck energy in the hips and pelvic area.

I then do some of the pelvic exercises. I love the pelvic tilts and usually do nine of these. As I do the first three, I take a deep breath, lift my hips off the bed, pull all the muscles in tight and with the out breath, I lower my hips and let out the sound AAAA. The next three are with the sound OOOO and the last three with the sound MMM.

I then do the exercise with moving my hips from side to side on the bed.

## Step 4 – Deep Breathing

I breathe deeply, so that my energy is flowing all round my body. I do this at regular times during the day.

### Step 5 – Delicious Shower

In the shower, as I soap my body, I tell myself "I am beautiful, I am lovely, my skin feels so soft and smooth." When I dry myself I take a moment to feel the softness of the towel against my skin and try to be gentle with drying myself.

### Step 6 – Coconut Oil Moisturise

I use mostly coconut oil on my skin and I like to make sure that every part of my skin is treated to some luxurious coconut oil. Depending on time, I might just massage and stroke my face in the morning and do a full body stroke in the evenings.

As I touch my skin, I use the sound "mmm" a lot. I love that one because it makes me feel really good.

### Step 7 - Inner Smile

I look in the mirror again and I might do the Inner Smile exercise, where I treat all of my organs to the energy of a smile.

### Step 8 – Clothes that make me feel good

I am then ready to get dressed and to put on clothes that really make me feel good.

### Step 9 – Sing and Laugh

If I am going out in the car I often start to sing some of my favourite songs as I go along. I make sure I have songs that make me laugh, so I can trigger off my Raucous Cackle!

### Step 10 – Pleasure all day

As I go about my day, I try to make everything into a sensuous, pleasure-filled experience. Use all of your senses. Really TASTE your food, FEEL the sensation of your clothes on your skin, LISTEN to things that uplift you and notice SMELLS that delight your senses. Surround yourself with things you like to LOOK at.

When you use all of your senses to appreciate the world around you, it reflects wonderful things back to you and you feel better as you go through your day. You are also more likely to notice the little ripple of orgasm in your body as she tells you she is experiencing pleasure throughout the day.

When you put YOU and YOUR PLEASURE as your NUMBER ONE PRIORITY, everything flows and everything works.

**Keeping My Sparkly Energies**

One of my favourite techniques to keep my energies bright and sparkly is to imagine that I am surrounding myself with a ball of white and golden light. This has the highest energy vibration and it allows only positive, love-based things and people to come into my space. Negativity tends to get dissolved on the way in or the ball of light returns it to the sender but with love attached. If any negativity does get through, the sting of it has often diminished because I am better equipped to deal with it.

With energy, the strongest energy always wins, so you can make sure that your energy is the highest in the room. This means you lift the energy of everyone else up to your level on the positive spiral, rather than allowing yourself to be pulled down to any negative place on the spiral that other people might occupy.

**Disconnect From the Energies of Others**

As you increase your orgasm energies, you tend to notice other people's negative energies less and less, as they just fall out of your awareness. Negative people tend not to be attracted to you anymore because a grand dose of your positivity might just ruin their day!

With the best will in the world, it is still very easy to pick up energies from other people and the world around you. This is why it is important to disconnect from those energies and keep your own energies pure, clean, bright and shiny. One of the best ways to do this is to imagine that you are sitting in the sun.

### Sit in the Sun

Breathe in the light and power of the Sun, mix this with your orgasm energy, and breathe out any dense, negative energies that no longer serve you. Imagine the flames of the sun are around you and, as you breathe out negativity, the fire vaporises it. There is nothing left to return back into your body or energy field.

### Universe and Earth Connection

Remember, It's All Connected! In managing your energies, balance is needed. It is important to be connected to the Universe, so that you can draw in ideas and inspiration. It is equally important to have your feet planted on the Earth, so that you can act on that inspiration and turn those ideas into reality.

When you are going out into the world of business, you need both. You need personal magnetism and the practicalities of being able to ask for the order and complete the paperwork accurately.

Here is a very powerful exercise that I use on a daily basis.

Imagine a stream of white and golden light coming down from the skies into the top of your head and down through your body. Breathe IN and draw it in and as you breathe OUT, imagine it flowing out of your feet and down into the Earth. With the next IN breath, draw that energy back up from the Earth and into your Body and on the OUT breath, imagine it going back out of the top of your head and out into the Universe.

You can run this energy around your body in a continuous loop.

Using your orgasm energy with the aid of these exercises will keep you soaring on the upward spiral of positivity.

# CHAPTER FIVE – HOW TO USE ORGASM ENERGY FOR INCREASED PROSPERITY

## From Orgasm to Prosperity

As you are now highly turned on as you go out into your work and business day, it is very possible that you are going to be more successful. That could translate into more money, which can then come back into the household money pot and buy lots of other wonderful things, thus bringing more pleasure to everyone.

This was certainly my experience. I went out into the world, sparkling with orgasmic energy and my business increased. I earned more money and worked less hours with less stress.

This led to me selling over £600,000 worth of products for the company I worked for and having days where I earned over £3000 in commissions for a couple of hours work.

All that started from a simple stroke of my clitoris.

So, ladies, use the fact that everything in the female brain and body is connected to everything else. Use it to exponentially explode your success from the introduction of a simple practice that increases your orgasms and multiplies your pleasure.

I would like to show you exactly how to use this material for increased prosperity in your business. When you regularly use Orgasm energy you can become more magnetic to people, opportunities and money.

Before I share with you all the marvellous ways in which you can use your Orgasm energy to increase your Prosperity, I would like to talk you to about Male and Female Energies.

## The Importance of Male and Female Energies for Creating and Manifesting

Men and women are quite different in how they manifest and create.

WHY does this matter to anyone, you might be thinking?

It is really the secret as to why men can often go straight for their goals and achieve them in exactly the way they envisioned them and women, who try the same methods, end up burned out.

When you understand these differences and how to balance these energies, you can operate much more from your natural feminine. This means you can create and manifest in a way that supports and nourishes you rather than drains you. This can give you more money and more success in much less time and with a lot less effort. This can free up your time to do things that really matter to you, instead of working all the time.

**How Men Get Goals**

Men operate a lot from their heads. Some of the qualities you often think of with male energies are focus, vision, clarity of thought and action, which are all important skills.

When we, as women, are taught to do goal setting, we are often trained how to do this from a male perspective. This is where everything is linear black and white and it is often about going out there, and bringing home the bounty. Not much has really changed from the days of the caveman going out hunting the sabre tooth tiger and bringing home the lunch- or the bacon- so to speak!

**Male Hunters and Female Receivers**

I remember when we went to Cresswell Crag, which is a limestone valley in Derbyshire, in the North of England. This area used to be an inland sea and early people would walk here from the area we now know as Northern France, to spend the winter here. There are caves located along the valley, which are underneath quite a high cliff.

The guide told us a story of how women would allow "lunch" to simply come to them, whilst the men were out busy hunting for a sabre tooth tiger. The children would go out with the men and they would look for the smaller, baby woolly mammoths. They would then chase them along the cliff top and manoeuvre them so they fell over the edge of the cliff top, which usually killed them on impact with the ground below. With good aim, that was straight into Mama's cooking pot!

Joking aside, that is how we as women manifest.

**How Women Create and Manifest**

Women have the ability to set an intention for something and then open themselves up to receive what they have asked for, or something better. That does not mean they just sit and wait for their request to be answered, although that can be the case. Most women tend to go out and do something in order to meet the Universe part way to bring their desired item to them.

As a woman, you create by drawing things into you, especially into your lower abdomen area, or the area that is your womb. It does not matter whether or not you physically have a womb, as the energetic imprint of that area is still there.

The womb is the area of physical and metaphysical creation, whether that is a baby, an idea or other manifestation. It will grow there until the time is right to give birth.

### Male Patterns Don't Work for Women

Males live in their heads. Women often try the same pattern, and end up feeling totally disconnected from their womb area. They try to connect with their heart energies, however frequently they don't drop their energies low enough into their bodies to really connect with their powerhouse of untapped resources.

As a woman, when you go out into the world of business and work, you spend most of your time operating from your masculine energies. Those are the energies of pushing forward, meeting deadlines and of making things happen. This often involves organising, controlling and running on adrenaline, which leads to stress.

We need an amount of this energy as that is what gets things done, however we can also balance that with our more feminine energies and accomplish great success.

### Feminine Energies

Women naturally operate in a completely different way from men, and this is not just in how men and women communicate with each other.

The more feminine energies tend to be kindness, caring and compassion. Women tend to be more nourishing and supportive than men and are more inclined towards co-operation rather than competition.

The purely feminine side often wants to spend the day singing, dancing, playing and having fun. This might include being at one with nature, playing games and being very creative. That has its place and we need to make time and space for that as women because it is what truly nourishes us.

**The Balance in Business**

For women in work and business, it is about finding that balance and oscillating between the two as necessary and appropriate.

Interestingly I have recently met a lot of women, who have left the corporate world to set up their own businesses. The common theme seems to be that women have got fed up with trying to succeed by using the traditional masculine ways of doing things.

Women no longer want to be playing power games or to be in competition with each other. They want to create wealth and success through co-operation and collaboration. In essence, they want to be WOMEN in BUSINESS, not women trying to operate by male rules. Women want to create and manifest success in their own way and by using their female abilities and energies.

Women want to work with each other to create amazing businesses. They are also more willing to partner up with the Universe to draw in more opportunities, rather than feeling like they have to control and manage everything, as they did in their previous corporate jobs. Women are ditching their square, angular power suits. They are opting for softer, more feminine curves. This brings flexibility and fluidity in everything they do, rather than rigid rules and straight lines. It is a more all-encompassing way of doing things and feels authentic.

### Energy Centres for Women

There are energy channels running up and down your body and there are seven main energy centres, called chakras, which are located between the root chakra, at the base of your spine and the crown chakra at the top of your head.

Of these seven energy centres, there are three which are crucial for women in business.

These are the Heart, the Solar Plexus and the Sacreal Centres.

# Chakra Points and Colours

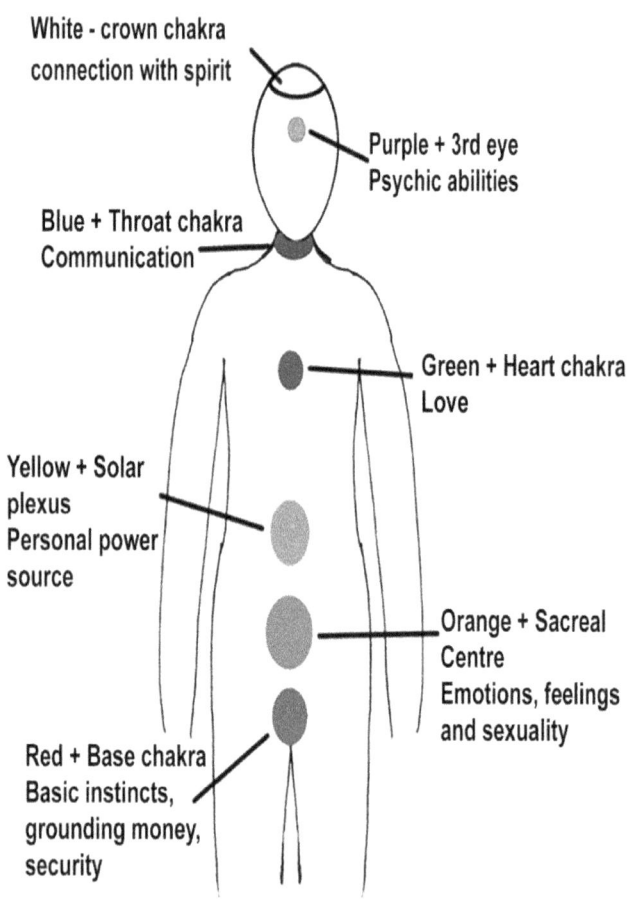

## Heart Centre

The first of these is the Heart Centre, which is located in the middle of your chest. It is often shown as a green colour and represents love in your life, including how you give and receive love. It also represents the love that you have for yourself.

## Heart-Centred Entrepreneur

You may have heard the term "heart-centred" entrepreneurs, which is mostly applied to women. This refers to women who do everything from a place of love for and service to other people. Coming from a place of love and passion is fantastic and needed, as long as there is a balance with other areas.

You can only really be "of service" to others when your own cup is filled and overflowing. When you give from that surplus of love and abundance, then everyone truly benefits. If you are giving wholeheartedly to others whilst you are in a place of personal depletion, that just leads to resentment. You can create magic and miracles in combination with other people, but you must remember to nourish yourself first.

## Solar Plexus

The second centre is called the solar plexus. This is located at the top of your lower abdomen, just below where your rib cage splits and just above your belly button. This is the seat of your personal power and is often depicted as yellow in colour.

## The Powerhouse for Sending Out Requests

This centre is important for manifesting and sending requests out into the Universe. It is the area that needs to be active for women to go out into the work and business world, and get things done. It is the centre that allows you to say NO, mean it and not feel guilty. When fully engaged, it is a powerful force to be reckoned with.

This is your core and needs to be strengthened. This is why exercises such as sit ups, the plank and pelvic tilts are very good for women because they physically strengthen those core muscles. When you need to find physical, emotional and spiritual strength, this is where it comes from. That is the time you need to be able to drop your energy out of your head and down into the physical core of your being and breathe from there.

**Sacreal Centre**

The third one is the sacreal centre, which is located below your belly button, in the area where your womb is or would be. This is often shown in Orange. It is the area of sex and emotions.

This is also the area where your greatest pleasure centres are located.

There are some simple exercises that you can do to stimulate the receiving abilities of the sacreal centre.

**The Gentle Art of Opening to Receive**

Drop your energies down into your body and breathe deeply in your abdomen. See how much stronger and more relaxed you feel. Notice how much more sensual and sexy you feel when your breathing is deep in your belly area.

You can focus your breathe in your vagina area and practise opening it, so it is ready to receive. Take a deep breath and tighten all the muscles of your vagina. As you release your breath, imagine the muscles letting go and the whole area starting to open up.

Try this with one finger inside your vagina. As you release your breath, what actually happens is that your finger is drawn further into your vagina.

You can try this tightening and releasing of your vagina muscles during sex. What you notice is that it creates huge amounts of pleasurable sensations. It also draws in the penis, finger, vibrator or whatever you might be using for your fun at the time. The vagina is opening to receive more pleasure, willingly and quite naturally.

Manifesting and creating your intentions works in the same way. When you have a wish for something, focus on creating it first in your womb area. Notice what it feels like in your body to already have that desire accomplished. Then, on an out-breath, you can fire it out of your body through your solar plexus, like sending an arrow out towards a target. Then open up your vagina to receive your goodies back in.

You can practise receiving in all areas of your life, such as receiving compliments, good stuff and help from other people. Practise saying yes to life in general.

## Breathing Through the Different Energy Centres for Success

You can breathe through different energy centres or a combination of centres, depending on what balance of energies you need to complete your tasks in the day. All you do is focus your attention on each centre and imagine that your breath is going in and out of that place on your body.

In my previous sales job, when I was driving a lot to see different customers, I would sit in my car and think about the upcoming appointment. I would breathe deeply in my sacreal (creation) centre for a few minutes to stimulate the female, attractive energy. I would then move my energies up to my solar plexus area and breathe deeply in this area. This was to fire up my personal power and to give me the structure and organisation to make sure I did my job properly. This included accurately completing the necessary paperwork for the orders.

I would project that positive energy forward to the customer's house, with the expectation of the customer buying from me.

Depending on the customer I was dealing with, I would use a greater or lesser degree of those energies. As an example, dealing with a man on his own might require me to be stronger, more confident and more assertive. On the other hand, dealing with a lady on her own might need a softer, more feminine approach, whilst still having enough personal power to complete the necessary business.

As I made my way home at the end of the day, my energies would be moving more into the feminine, as I thought about the remainder of the evening with my husband and the pleasure that was going to bring me.

If you know you are going into a tough business environment, where perhaps the atmosphere is not likely to be pleasant, then you can spend some time breathing your energies through your heart centre. When you flow love energy at a difficult situation or person, this can soften things up considerably and make the situation much easier to deal with. That does not mean that you give in to all the demands of others or allow yourself to be treated like a doormat. It means you bring the feminine energies of love, compassion and co-operation to the table, in order to create a win-win situation for everyone – you included!

### Thinking Points

Notice whether your energies seem to be more masculine oriented and focused on action, reaching targets and making stuff happen or whether they are more feminine in nature, which are co-operation, intuition and receiving.

Notice how you feel with this current balance and see how you could turn the dial to incorporate more feminine qualities into your day.

Practise breathing into each of the three main energy centres and move your focus from one to another, so you can notice the shift from more love-based, to feeling more powerful, to feeling more receptive. You can also do this in reverse or simply focus on each one individually.

**CHAPTER SIX – ORGASMIC GOALS AND INTENTIONS**

When you allow yourself to shine out into the world, you can accomplish anything you put your mind to, in less time, with less effort and less stress.

When you are all powered-up and ready to go, it really does help to have a BIG project or goal to channel that immense energy into.

Before you start any goal setting type exercises, get your Orgasmic energy running around your body, so that you are sending your wishes and desires out into the Universe with a super-turbo-charged powerhouse behind them.

Ask yourself, "What does your Ideal Day and your Ideal Career look like?" "If you had all the money and time in the world, what would you love to do?" "If you knew you could not fail, what big dream would you pursue?"

It is often said that the biggest factor in manifesting intentions and achieving desires is the WHY? This is why do you want what you want?

When your WHY is big enough, important enough and juicy enough, then the HOW, which is "How do I accomplish that?" is the secondary thing.

You need to have an overall direction of where you want to go, then take the first action steps towards that dream. The rest of the HOW then unfolds for you as you go along. It shows up in the form of the right people and opportunities just at the perfect moment, exactly as you need them. Often all you have to do is to say YES to them and take advantage of them.

Are your goals orgasm-worthy? Or are they a bit flat and lifeless?

When you think about your WHY, it should generate the same level of excitement and anticipation in your body as the thought of hot, steamy sex with the most desirable person of your dreams. This is like being head over heels in love, and having a massive chemistry with your goals. When you physically feel that energy in your body, you are well on your way to magnetically attracting all your goals – in true female style!

**Dream Bigger**

After an Orgasm, this is a time when really big goals and dreams often pop into your head, as you have the confidence to believe you can conquer the world and do anything you choose to do. Remember your notebook and pen!

These big dreams are frequently accompanied by a complete action plan of what you need to do to accomplish them. If the plan is not complete, then it usually has the first few steps that you need to take. These will be very clear to you.

The size and scale of these projects might take you by surprise. It is important to write them down before your "rational" mind kicks in and starts telling you why these things are too big or too scary or can't be done. These ideas have come straight from your Highest Self, via your body. As such these are the true guidance of what you are capable of doing. All you need to do is to take the first steps.

**Biggest Thing to Accomplish**

Right after an orgasm, ask yourself, "What is the biggest thing I am here on this planet to accomplish?" and wait for an answer.

You might be surprised!

Then ask yourself, "What else is possible?" and you will probably find there is something even bigger behind it that is just waiting for the space to emerge.

Whatever it is, take immediate action. Intentions powered by Orgasm are like rocket fuel and the Universe loves them!

### Draw Things to You

Think about what you desire, drop your energies into your abdomen and feel it as already accomplished. Then imagine that you are firing it out of your solar plexus, (which is the point just below your rib cage) with the instructions to bring you back opportunities and money. Make sure that part of the request includes drawing in the right and perfect people who can help you with accomplishing your dreams.

Send out an energy ball of white and golden light to attract those people and draw them back into your space, almost like a magnet.

### Attracting Your Ideal Clients and Customers

When you are vibrating with orgasmic energy, it is much easier to attract your ideal clients to you. Orgasm energy acts as a very clear filter for people, who are either attracted to you and your work or repelled.

Those clients that are drawn to you are likely to be people like you, who share your values and are fun to work with. That makes doing business much easier. Your clients have a similar energy to you and it can feel like doing business with yourself. It really is a case of like attracts like. Those clients are also more likely to stay with you over a longer period of time and buy from you frequently. They will be delighted to recommend you to their friends.

**CHAPTER SEVEN – OTHER BENEFITS TO USING YOUR ORGASM ENERGY**

## Rapid Success and Amazing Results

So, what is likely to happen when you turn on your orgasm energy and go out in the world, shining brightly and magnetic to people, opportunities and money?

It is important to know the impact that you are likely to create, so that you can be prepared for the consequences of those actions, positive or negative and you remain in control of your energies and your body.

When you start to shine brightly out into the world, fantastic things are likely to start to happen to you, new opportunities will show up for you, new friends will appear in your life and money is likely to increase.

You are more willing to take bigger, bolder and more courageous actions than you have ever taken, which naturally leads to bigger and better results. You are more able to tap into the intuition and insights that come from the wisdom in your body and to be in the right place at the right time to take advantage of opportunities.

This can be amazing and can happen very quickly.

## Success too Fast

On the flip side of this, success can come faster and easier than you have ever experienced and there can be a danger of shutting it all off. This is commonly called a Sabotage Pattern, and can be as a result of many old patterns, including the ideas that success is hard and can only come as a result of pain and struggle. The best antidote to this is to keep experiencing the pleasure of Orgasms!

### Orgasm Energy in the Workplace

Not everyone has their own business. Indeed even business owners can feel like employees at times. You may work with people very similar to yourself and sometimes you have to work with colleagues who can be a drain. Orgasm energy will keep you positive and help you to work better with co-workers and keeps you safe from any negativity.

### Draw in Genuine People

People using orgasm energy tend to be open, authentic and congruent. This is because the energy is genuine and is there nowhere to hide. People show up as who they truly are. They are in integrity with themselves and their products and services. What you see is what you get and that is a consistent message.

### Be Lucky and Be in the Right Place at the Right Time

As you use your orgasm energy more and more, you find you start to become luckier. You are more likely to find yourself in exactly the right place at the most auspicious time, having a conversation with the perfect person that can help you with your business or your career.

That is partly your intuition guiding you. It is also due to the personal magnetism and charisma that comes from your increased Orgasm energy.

**Visualisations for Success**

While you are in this high energy place, with orgasmic energy running round your body, this is a good time to think about any upcoming presentations or meetings that you need to attend. It is important to see these as being a win-win for everyone. Set up an EXPECTATION of a positive result, that flows easily to a YES. This is done by getting a picture in your mind of the desired outcome and feeling the energy and joy of that success.

**Pre Meeting Insight**

Before you go into a meeting or pick up the phone to talk to someone, breathe deeply into your belly and ask yourself, "How can I best serve this customer?" and "What would be useful for me to know in order to get the right outcome for everyone?" Listen quietly for the answers.

You can be aware of that information as you go to deal with that person and use it accordingly to create the most appropriate all round solution.

## Intuition

According to the Oxford English Dictionary, Intuition is described as,

*"The ability to understand something instinctively, without the need for conscious reasoning."*

The Origin of the word is Late Middle English (denoting spiritual insight or immediate spiritual communication) and from late Latin *intuitio(n-)*,
from Latin *intueri* 'consider'

## Intuition of Situations and People

Intuition is that sense of just knowing whether something is right or not for you. It is mostly a sensation in the body, usually in the digestive tract, or gut. This is the reason why intuition is often called a "gut feeling".

Intuition can give you a strong sense that it is absolutely right to go forward with a course of action, however illogical it might seem. That feeling assures you that everything will be OK and will more than likely turn out better than you could have expected. This also applies to people, where you feel an immediate positive connection to someone.

Likewise intuition can steer you away from disastrous or potentially dangerous situations. This is especially important where everything maybe looks good on the surface and there is no logical reason why you should not go forward. Yet some part of you feels very uncomfortable and you are hesitant to continue.

This can be equally true of people. It can be a warning that something is not quite right and you should proceed with caution in dealing with them. It can be very hard to say exactly what that is, especially if the outward appearances do not give any reason for a lack of trust.

**Clarity of Thought**

One of the big benefits of powering up your orgasm energies is the clarity of thought it brings you. In the calm afterglow of an orgasm, you can have more profound insights into your life and business that at any other time.

## Creative Problem Solving

When you have a challenge you want to solve, write it down on a piece of paper. I would suggest you write it out as your desired outcome. As an example, this might be something like "How can I double my income, working half as many hours?"

Write as many possible answers as you can think of. Leave blank space on the paper and the pen on top of the paper. Then go and have an orgasm – or a few orgasms, if it is a really big problem – and see what creative ideas pop into your head. After your orgasm, write down any insights you have received. You will know they are the right ones because they will feel perfect to you.

A few years ago I created a meditation called "Creative Problem Solver." This can be used in conjunction with Orgasm energy.

While you are still in a reflective space after your orgasm, switch on the audio and go straight into the deep, peaceful relaxation. This will give your mind and body chance to really work together to give you the most powerful answers to your challenge.

When you come back, you will have a sense that you know exactly what you need to do.

## Combine an Orgasm Power Up with Coaching Questions for Fantastic Insights

A great way to get insights or answers to problems is by asking yourself some powerful questions. You can ask the question of "What might the likely outcome be, if I pursue this path?" The answer is based on your current thoughts and feelings about that path. It also reflects the actions you are currently taking or not. The answer is not set in stone and will change as soon as you make any changes in thought, word and deed.

I did this exercise with a friend of mine when we were looking at a number of options for the direction of her business. Her energy was quite heavy because she was feeling overwhelmed and confused, so she was not thinking straight.

I asked her what options she was considering. Before she told me, I asked her to think about a hot, sexy tumble under the sheets with her partner, especially one where she had experienced lots of fun, pleasure and orgasms. Her face flushed and she started to giggle. Then suddenly she blurted out her top three choices for her business.

As we had narrowed them down to three, it made it easier to look at each one. Before each one, I asked her to think back to her orgasm state. This was so that the answers were coming directly from her body and from her highest energy place.

"Naughty" words like "sex and orgasm" broke the chatter patterns in her mind, got her energies out of her head and down into her body. This meant she was open to receive much clearer answers to her questions. We ended up back at the place that her own intuition and heart had told her to do, over a year ago. She had ignored this wisdom because she had unfortunately got caught up in "guru-itis," where she felt that other so-called "experts" knew more about what was best for her and her business than her own body wisdom.

### Conversation Starter

When you are radiating with orgasmic energy, people want to know who you are and what you do. People are drawn to your energy and want to come and speak to you. It gives you an opportunity to start a conversation with someone and have their undivided attention, even if that is just for a few minutes.

If you can stride confidently into a room and light up that room with positivity, you will very soon be surrounded by a group of willing listeners.

**Be Remembered**

Be different.

Be the one with the bright energy and the bright clothes.

Be the one that brings laughter, fun and playfulness to the conversation.

Be the one that is the outrageous flirt – with the clear boundaries!

People buy from people they like. If you can be the one that really causes a person to feel good about themselves, their lives and their business, they will buy your product or service because that will remind them about how good you made them feel.

## CHAPTER EIGHT – POSITIVE CHANGES IN YOU AS A PERSON

### Positive Changes in You

As you increase your orgasm energy and shine that out into the world, you are going to be showing up as a different person.

This is the person that you really are at the core of your being, with all the limitations removed.

Some of the positive, empowering changes you might notice happening are the following:

You are more powerful, because you feel in control of your own body and your own pleasure. Your self-love, self-acceptance and self-esteem will go through the roof. Your self-belief will increase. You know what you want and confidently expect to receive it. You know what you need to do to accomplish your dreams and you have the courage to take bold action steps towards those goals.

You are unlikely to be willing to tolerate any crap and silly nonsense from anyone, whether that is in the workplace or from people trying to pull you down.

You respect yourself and you set clear boundaries with other people, in all areas of your life, as to what is acceptable behaviour towards you and what is not.

You will probably find yourself feeling more feminine and more willing to embrace those womanly aspects. You become more willing to drop your energies down into your body and really live from that female place. This leads to you listening to your own wisdom and trusting in yourself and your abilities, rather than relying on the opinions of others.

You find you become much more resourceful and creative because you are more able to access your natural intuition and guidance system.

You reach out to others for help when you need it, whilst being willing to decline or accept advice as it feels right to you.

As you become more at ease with yourself, it allows you to connect with other people at a much deeper level because you feel whole and complete as a human being.

When you shine powerfully out into the world, it highlights the genuine authenticity of who you really are. This means that masks and pretence are likely to fall away, you have less desire to "create an impression," so you project only one persona out into the world – that is the true you.

Your sense of humour shows up more frequently. You become more playful, so you take yourself and your business less seriously. This often leads to getting a lot more done in much less time, with better results.

With more orgasmic pleasure, you naturally start to value yourself more in all areas of your life. Your self-worth increases dramatically. You begin to treat yourself like a Queen, instead of a second class citizen. Negative stuff, such as guilt and shame, falls away as you allow yourself to enjoy more and more pleasure.

You start to put your own needs and requirements FIRST. When you do that, things start to work in wonderful ways for you. This means that people-pleasing has to go. You become a mistress of the fine art of saying NO to people and things that drain you or do not nourish you.

Likewise this increases your ability to say YES to the things that you desire. You become open and willing to receive them because you know you deserve them.

You approach collaboration and co-operation from a win-win place and that includes you. The words ME TOO and ME FIRST start to show up in your vocabulary.

You become less inclined to be bothered to look at negative stuff in order to see what might be stopping you. This means you just get on with doing what you want to do. You have tools in your toolbox to deal with negativity or sabotage patterns, as they arise in the moment. When something does come up that potentially could drag you down, you are more likely to reach for pleasure than wallow in pain. This keeps you on the upward spiral of positivity.

## The Positive Power of Orgasm Energy

You cannot have the amazing energies of orgasm and pleasure running through your body at the same time as feelings of unworthiness, shame or other negative feelings. The two things have completely different energy vibrations and cannot inhabit the same space in your body. One or the other has to go. You can choose your new-found pleasure energy or continue with your pain. Most women tend to prefer the pleasure. This means the pain starts to evaporate because it no longer has your attention.

## CHAPTER NINE – SEXUAL HEALING

### Sexuality and Sexual Healing

Powering up your Orgasm energies and using them in the world could bring up any negative beliefs you might have about yourself, your sexuality and your own power as a woman.

DISCLAIMER: I am not a medical person or a counsellor, so if you have any mental, physical or emotional trauma related to sexual issues, please seek professional help before stirring it up.

You might find yourself bursting into tears at the end of a fantastic orgasm and have no clue why you are now crying your eyes out.

The reason for the tears is that you have just released off some pain or trauma from the past that related to you or your sexuality. Sometimes healing can take place without really needing to look too deeply at the issues behind the pain. Your "She-Body" did not feel it was appropriate for you to know what it was or for you to delve into it. Just know that something major shifted and released.

This has happened to me on several occasions. I would suddenly feel a huge sadness sweep over me with waves of uncontrollable tears. I would cry until I felt like I could cry no more and then, as suddenly as it started, it stopped and was gone. When I tried to question my body and mind what it was all about, I got a firm response from my body of "I am not telling you. It's none of your business. It's all gone now, so go and enjoy your day."

**Feeling for Healing**

If you are experiencing intense negative emotions and feelings, then just allow yourself to be with them. You don't necessarily need to go into the details of the story of what happened. Just let those feelings be in your body. Observe them, let them do whatever they want to do and let that carry on - without any judgement – until it all subsides. Once those emotions have been fully felt and processed, they leave! They really do!

So what this means is that, if you feel the desire to cry, then let yourself do that until you cannot cry any more. All the events and memories that have that same energy can be completed and released at the same time.

If you are feeling intense anger, then that is often better expressed in a physical way. This might be something like thumping a pillow as hard as you can and shouting out all the obscene words you can think of in relation to the offending person or situation. There comes a point where you will probably collapse on the floor laughing. Yes, nice girls do kick back, even if it is just a pillow or all in your head!

## Forgiveness

It is very important to forgive, both yourself and other people. The past has gone and cannot be changed.

Forgiveness does not mean forgetting and it does not mean condoning any wrongdoings that other people may have done to you. It is purely a selfish act of letting go of the emotional charge around an incident or situation, so that you can be free of the pain of it.

Whilst you are carrying that negativity around in your system, it is you that it is affecting more than anyone else. At some point those emotions will need to be released in order for you to be able to truly shine your light out into the world. Seek professional help if necessary.

## Stimulate Your Own Orgasm

The more aware you become of what creates pleasure in your own body, the more you can use this to stimulate your own orgasm, which opens up the whole womb area.

## Womb and Ovary Healing

It is very powerful to heal this area of your body because it is a place where past trauma may have been stored. The womb can contain a lot of negative feelings and emotions around you as a woman, your sexuality and your feelings about sex. There is a lot of research on this subject, which is way beyond the scope of this book.

I would like to share my own experiences and the exercises I used to help myself.

## Healing the Space Left by the Removal of a Dysgerminoma Tumour

In May 1988, at age 21, I was diagnosed with a malignant ovarian tumour called a Dysgerminoma. This was the size of a small melon, about 2 lbs/ 1 kg in weight and all contained within its own skin. When I finally got to see the Consultant, he was quite horrified at the size of it and was very concerned that it was about to burst. He operated on me to remove it less than 48 hours later.

He was an amazing surgeon and told me that, because of my age, he had managed to leave virtually all of my internal reproductive organs intact– apart from one of my ovaries. This had had to come out because the dysgerminoma had been attached to it, however, he assured me, that I would still be able to have children. This I did in 1994 and 1996 and I was very proud of myself because I managed not to tear any of my vaginal muscles as I gave birth to my two beautiful daughters.

The surgeon performed the operation in such a way that I did not lose any of my ability to feel pleasure.

I had not realised that this removal of my ovary had left an energetic hole, as well as a physical gap.

During a meditation a few years ago, I had a very profound healing experience where it felt like I was drawing the energy of that missing ovary back into my body and re-integrating it with the rest of my womanly parts. I also found that I had been holding quite a bit of trauma and stress in the scar that ran right across my abdomen from one side to the other. This needed to be released and it felt wonderful to have a sense of wholeness and completeness again.

The following exercise is one of the things that I did as part of that healing process.

### Golden Light Visualisation for Lovingly Cleansing and Healing the Womb Area

Imagine holding a sponge that is full of golden light and using it to clean around the inside of your womb area – or the space where that would be. Clean the whole area with the sponge including any tubes, your ovaries and down into your vagina. When the sponge becomes full of negative energies and emotions, you can just wring it out or throw it away and get a new one.

## Sexual Energy – My Story

Over the years, I had come to realise that I did not like myself very much. I had poor self-esteem and low self-worth. I would never have considered myself a sensual and sexual woman.

I had seen this as a blockage when I had lost over 5 stone (70lbs/30kg) in weight over the previous two years. I identified one of the biggest fears as follows, "What if I lose all this weight, and I am walking down the street in a short skirt and tight top, shining brightly because I feel amazing and some bloke whistles at me or worse, makes some inappropriate suggestion – and I can't say NO!???"

I had shut this energy down, as many women have, because I felt it was unsafe to display it. This, however, is the paradox. Our sensual, sexual energy is who we are, it is one of the primary driving forces in the Universe and is the energy of creation and manifesting – and that is not just babies!

## From Skinny Dipping to Naked Sauna

In 2003 I went to Hawaii on a self-help seminar. I was "persuaded" to go skinny dipping in the hot tub with the rest of the members of the group. I did not really want to do it, as I loathed myself and my body. I felt really uncomfortable and wanted to curl up in a corner and die, but nevertheless I took off my clothes and got in the hot tub. This was not helped when I came home and told my husband about the incident, to which his remark was, "So, why won't you go skinny dipping with me?" This all had a huge dose of guilt and shame attached to it!

I had long forgotten this incident, until we went on holiday to Laax in Switzerland at the end of February 2014. The hotel had a beautiful spa. It also had a mixed sauna and steam room, and these had a "no swimming costumes or clothes" rule.

Greg suggested that we went in there and I found I was actually quite OK with that. This surprised me as much as it surprised him. For the first time in my life, I was quite happy with my body and with being a naked woman in the presence of other naked men and women. I approached the whole exercise with a spirit of openness and curiosity, which had never happened to me before.

I also found that as summer approached, I was more willing to go out in public in a short skirt or tight shorts. That was another thing that had never happened to me – ever! I became able to accept compliments, from both women and men. I have been able to create my own boundaries of what is or is not acceptable behaviour. I have learnt that my body is mine and I have every right to say no to unwelcome attention.

I have been able to release feelings of shame around me and my sexuality, along with feelings of not being good enough. This has allowed me to enjoy being a woman.

OP-ing and the pleasure from regular orgasms had shifted my view of myself from a place of self-loathing to one of self-acceptance and self-love. This was without me giving it any conscious thought or effort. It just happened.

## CHAPTER TEN – THE DOWNSIDES AND WARNINGS!

### Setting Personal Boundaries

When you start to increase your sexual energies, it is vital to set personal boundaries.

When you are shining brightly and oozing orgasmic energy, you will attract attention from people, both of same sex and of the opposite sex.

You are likely to get all sorts of offers from all sorts of people for all sorts of things. Some of these will be positive and totally amazing. Some will be at the opposite end of the scale.

Unfortunately, not everyone will be pleased to see the sparkling, new you and, sadly, some people will try to pull you down and stop you in your tracks.

This is more about them and their insecurities than it is about you.

Don't judge or be frightened. Decide what you want from those people and encounters.

It is vitally important for you to be clear on what is, and what is not, acceptable behaviour from other people. And you can say NO!

When you sparkle with Orgasmic Energy, your vibration is high and your whole energy field is very open as this is part of receiving wonderful things.

It is essential that you have very strong, clear boundaries, so that you are in control of who and what you let into your personal space.

Put up your boundaries, put yourself inside your own bubble of golden light protection and try to stay away from negative people. Don't let their opinions, comments, judgements and actions spoil your energy or steal your dreams.

As you sparkle with Orgasmic Energy, you may find that some of your family, current friends and work colleagues support you and others don't. You may well find yourself with a new circle of friends.

Say Yes to the people and things that truly resonate with you and confidently say No to what does not feel right or good to you.

Remember YOU are in control and YOU decide!

## Protect your Energies

Here are some of my favourite techniques to keep my own energies bright and sparkly and to protect me from other energy-vampires.

### White Light

Imagine yourself wrapped in a big bubble of white light. Imagine it is all round you, including around your feet and head and see it stretching about 3-4 feet (1-1.5m) metres beyond yourself.

### Golden Light

Even more powerful is a bubble of Golden Light because it allows love and good things into your energy field and converts negative energy back into positive and returns it to the sender as positive energy and Love.

### Mirrors – Word of Warning!

Some people will advise you to use a mirror to return any negative energy to the sender. If you do this, simply return the energy to the sender that has been sent to you – do not increase the intensity with which it goes back, as that can set up a very destructive cycle of energy and negative actions.

## Turning Your Energy Dial Up and Down

Your personal energy is like a dial, which can be turned up or down, depending on the circumstances.

You can shine like a lighthouse beacon, where you are sexy, confident and incredibly magnetic to people and opportunities. This is perfect if you want to attract a new client or new business.

You can also turn your energy down, so you are almost invisible. This can be very useful if you are walking in a dark street or poorly lit car-park at night and you don't want anyone to see you.

To be noticed, stand up straight, breathe deeply from your abdomen, feel the energy running up and down your body and feel your personal power. Think of yourself as a Rainbow of bright colours and sparkling light. Remember to Smile.

To be invisible, imagine you are turning down a dial in your abdomen, so that you turn down the energy and the colours go to black and white or even grey. You can also imagine a cloak of invisibility around you, so you go unnoticed.

Keep yourself safe. Don't put yourself in danger with your new-found Orgasm energies.

## What Stops Women from Using their Orgasm Energy?

There are numerous answers to this question, ranging from personal beliefs to cultural conditioning, fear of what others might say up to fear of personal safety.

I will briefly mention a few of the most common things. Some of them can be changed by a simple acknowledgement that they exist, others might require coaching or counselling to move through them. Please seek appropriate help as necessary.

Women have been trained from being little girls to shut off their sexual and orgasmic energies.

When these things are brought into awareness and questioned, it gives you the opportunity to make new and empowered choices for yourself.

### Observation exercise

As you read the list, just notice what comes up for you and how you feel.

Have a curious attitude of "That's interesting. I wonder who that belongs to? Does it serve me to hold onto that? Could I let that go? What might be a more supportive belief for me to take on board?" Most of this stuff is old conditioning that comes from family and society and is not even yours!

**Feeling for healing**

One of the most powerful things you can do with old stuff is just allow it to come to the surface, be with the emotions that come with and let yourself feel them in your body.

Chances are these are old emotions that occurred at some point in time and were never full processed at the time. They now need to be completed. Observe them without judgement and let them just move through your body. When you let your body fully process these emotions, then they subside and they are gone.

**Grounding and Connecting**

Feel yourself connected and grounded into the earth by some deep roots that come out of your feet and go straight down into the centre of the earth. This keeps you safe as you are doing processing work and also allows old beliefs to drain away, whilst bringing in powerful energies from the Earth and the Universe to carry you forward.

**Whatever works for you**

Feel free to use and adapt any of my suggested processes or use your own favourite energy clearing method. It does not matter what you use, as long as it is something you feel comfortable with – and it works for you!

**Pleasure Preventers**

Some of the most common reasons that women don't allow themselves to experience orgasms and the pleasure that can come from that are the following:

### Shame

This is probably the biggest one of the lot. In our society, women are shamed for being female and many women have experienced shame over their bodies, shame over their sexuality, shame over desiring things – especially money and material things – and often shame over being YOU.

### Judgement

We are taught from a young age to be judgemental about everything, so everything has a label of good or bad and right or wrong. This applies to money, people, ourselves and the world in general.

### Unsafe to shine

This is where it is unsafe to be pretty, clever, rich or unique in any way and many women have experiences where they shut off these wonderful energies because they feel unsafe.

### Shining too Brightly

If you ever heard any of the following phrases as a child, then it quite likely that you have toned down your natural exuberance and natural personality, in order to fit in with the world around you:

"She's got a mind of her own, she's a "proper little madam", a handful, she is always in trouble, she's disruptive, she's a tomboy, needs a firm hand" and so on.

This causes you to apologise for yourself, for your energy and for who you are because you have been made to feel that you are wrong because of who you are, so you shrink inwards, close up, tone it down in order to conform and be accepted as one of the obedient crowd.

**Fear of Visibility**

This for many women has led to having a fear of being visible and being seen. Women try to hide, not to stand out, they try not to be any bigger or better or more successful than other people as someone might get upset and harm them in some way. The tricky thing with this point is that we hide ourselves so well that money and success can't see us either!

**Family and Society Conditioning**

Family and society experiences and conditioning plays a huge part in why women shut off their sexual and orgasmic energies. Look at the patterns of your family in relation to sexuality and success. See how many of those you have maybe taken on board as your own.

## People Pleasers

Women have been trained to be "people-pleasers" that is to put everyone else and their needs first and us, as women, last. This comes back to the idea that we are here to serve others and the idea of service to others often involves sacrifice of the self.

When we put ourselves first, we often hear the word "selfish" being used, and this is generally with a tone of voice that suggests that "selfish" is a bad thing. Actually it is not, because you can only really give to other people when you have first nourished and taken care of yourself.

## Opinions of others

Being over-concerned about the opinions of other people is often closely connected with not trusting yourself and your own judgement.

## Blaming others and not taking personal responsibility

This is the flip side of looking towards others for approval and validation. It is blaming others or external circumstances for your situation or looking for someone to save you.

To be truly successful you have to be able to take full responsibility for yourself and your actions, so you take the credit for the things that go well for you and also accept the consequences of your own actions, when things don't turn out as planned.

## Pleasure is bad

Linked in with this is the whole idea that pleasure is a bad thing and especially sexual pleasure, which really should be confined to the bedroom and should certainly not be linked to practical things like "work and making money," which are supposed to hard and difficult and as far away from pleasure as you could imagine.

## Bad Girl Syndrome

Part of this is the "Bad Girl" syndrome, when you have been caught "playing" or "having pleasure" or "goofing off" when you "should" be working or doing something more constructive! Maybe as a little girl, you were caught exploring your own body and discovering what gave you pleasure – and were severely punished and shamed for it? Or worse your brother or male cousin or male friend, who was with you at the time was given a pat on the back for being a "good, big, boy" and you were punished for being a "bad girl?"

## Guilt and Should Conditioning

The weapon of choice most used against women when they try to put themselves first and stop people-pleasing is another biggie – Guilt!

Should or Should not conditioning often comes into play as well, as other people tell women how to think, feel, act and how to live their lives. People around you will usually have an opinion about sexuality and pleasure, how that should or should not operate and what "the rules" are about that.

## Lack of Self Worth and Not Good Enough

All this leads to a feeling of a lack of self-worth, of not being good enough or worthy of anything very much and a feeling of total powerlessness.

## Fear of Rejection, Betrayal and Abandonment

Underneath that can also be the threat or fear that if you don't comply with other people's wishes, then you might be rejected, betrayed, abandoned or have the love, support and friendship of family and friends withdrawn.

## Fear of Personal Power

Power can be a concept that women have trouble with, especially when it comes in the same sentence as money because it can throw up some very negative connotations.

In our history, it has been difficult for a woman to be powerful, especially in having her own money – and be safe! It is only in the last century that women have been allowed to earn, have and keep their own money. In the past, women were controlled and shamed. They were the property of their fathers and husbands. Outspoken, confident, courageous women were often disposed of in one way shape or form.

### Orgasm Power Up for a Big Clearing

One of the quickest ways to draw limiting beliefs and blockages to the surface is to treat yourself to a Pleasurable Orgasm Power Up before you even start working on anything negative or challenging. Intense pleasure often brings up all the "should and should nots," fears and limiting beliefs at the same time.

The longer your pleasure continues, the more likely the pleasure will override any negative emotions – if you allow it do to that! If you do this clearing and releasing work from a high energy place, then a lot of the old issues simply fade into insignificance. That means feeling it in your body and not just intellectualising it in your mind!

You cannot have the feelings of immense, orgasmic pleasure running in your body at the same time as a lack of self-worth or any other limitation. They have a completely different energy and they cannot run at the same time. It is one or the other. The good thing is you get to choose. When you have allowed yourself to experience enough pleasure in your body, pleasure soon starts to win!

All the other, non-serving stuff simply has to go because there is not room for it in your body.

Most limitations and blockages are dense, heavy energies that no longer serve you. When you increase the levels of pleasure in your body, these old energies have to simply fall away because they are vibrationally incompatible with the high-energy pleasure energies. They can no longer be a part of your physical, spiritual or energetic make-up.

This is the power of ADDING IN PLEASURE and ORGASM Energy, rather than trying to remove limiting beliefs and blockages.

Let Pleasure become your preferred choice!

## Other Healing and Coaching

I had an interesting experience during a coaching session, where I was being coached. We were looking at old limiting beliefs and patterns and processing them with a mixture of touch on my head and verbal clearing phrases.

I suddenly felt a huge surge of jealousy rise up in my body, along with strong memories around the person it related to. It was not something I had been expecting to find. As I continued with the verbal processing, my body suddenly went into orgasm.

I felt the energy start in my genitals and shoot up and down my body. It was very strange to be feeling strong jealousy and intense orgasm in my body at the same time.

I told my coach what was happening and she encouraged me to be with both and just let both happen, without trying to change or stop either. She carried on with the verbal processing and encouraged me to let the orgasm energy push all the other stuff out of my body.

As the orgasm deepened and my body contractions intensified, my breathing slowed down, I felt my face flush and I felt the oxytocin and serotonin flood through my body and I felt calm. I lay in the chair physically shaking and then started laughing as the orgasm subsided.

When I looked inside, the jealousy had gone. That has got to be one of the strangest healing sessions I have had. It was totally unexpected.

My body knew exactly what I needed. As I had been working with orgasm energy, my body also knew that I would know what was happening and would not be frightened by the process, so she could use that for healing.

We cleared the negativity at every level – mentally, spiritually, emotionally and physically. With the physical reactions of the orgasm, it moved that energetic imprint and memory out of every part of my being.

It also deepened my conviction that you cannot have the powerful, positive feelings and emotions associated with orgasm in your body at the same time as intense negativity. It is one or the other, as they are totally different vibrations at every level.

Having spent many years wallowing about in negative emotions and memories in trying to help clients clear limiting beliefs, blasting them out through orgasm energy is a more pleasurable and fun way to undergo personal growth. Interestingly those old feelings don't seem to come back.

## Dealing with Fear

Most of what stops women from moving forward and taking the next big step in life is FEAR, which is False Expectations Appearing Real.

If you are experiencing fear, it is likely that you will be having a physical reaction in your body.

Notice your fear. Just observe it.

## Collapse Old Beliefs with Orgasm Energy

1. Then get yourself into a really high, orgasmic state. Feel the light, bright, joyful energy running around your body. Breathe deeply into your abdomen and imagine you are going to play the most awesome, exciting game of your life. Take your energies as high as you can, stand tall and feel yourself glowing and shining.
2. Then switch back to your fear as quickly as possible. The trick to this is to move as rapidly as possible between the two states.
3. Now you have an experience of both an ORGASMIC state and a state of FEAR. Which feels better to you?
4. From the place of fear, stand up straight, breathe, smile and go back to Orgasmic state.

5. From orgasmic energy, TRY (and that is a very key word) to go back to FEAR. It is quite hard to do.
6. Switch rapidly a couple of times from orgasmic state to fear state and notice how much harder it is each time to access the fear state.
7. Try to access the old fears and beliefs again. You may well find that they have gone, or at least the emotional sting has gone.
8. This is an important distinction because there may be a message for you of things (or people) that you do need to approach with caution. It is more empowering to approach these potential challenges from a place of calm and logic, so that you can actually deal with the issues.
9. It is crucial at this point, whilst you are still in an orgasmic state, to take some action based on the new beliefs. The quicker you take action, the quicker those beliefs of "I CAN" become anchored in your mind and body.

**CHAPTER ELEVEN IT'S ALL CONNECTED! HOORAY!**

## How to live life in an upward spiral of Pleasure

Understanding the structure of your female brain is a vitally important factor for you to live a life of pleasure.

Studies have shown that men and women's brains operate in very different ways. It is often said that men are able to concentrate on only one thing at a time, such as their work or money. Everything else, such as personal relationships, is put to one side until it becomes relevant.

I have seen the structure of male and female brains explained in terms of boxes. A woman's brain has everything in one box, where everything is connected to everything else. A man, on the other hand, has divided this into many boxes, where, ideally everything is separate from everything else.

In both cases, only one box can be accessed at any one time.

This is fantastic information for women and is the key to a successful, pleasure-filled life of abundance and prosperity!

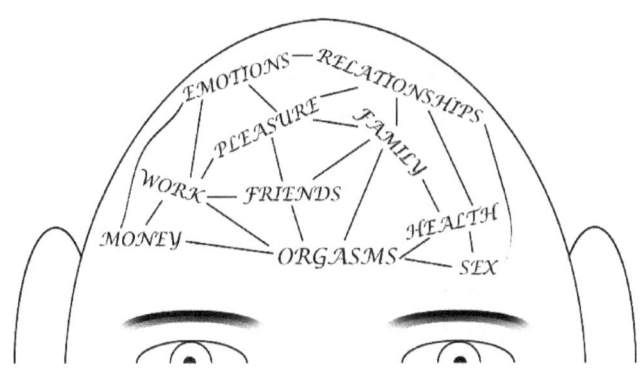

**Everything is Connected to Everything Else!**

When you feel amazing about yourself that reflects in every area of your life.

You are more in tune with your body and its needs, so you naturally choose foods that support your health. You are more likely to take regular exercise to keep those orgasm energies flowing around your body.

When you take better care of yourself, you have more energy and your physical body is more able to support you in anything that you want to do.

When you experience the pleasure of regular orgasms, you become turned on from the inside out. You are lit up like a bright, shining beacon and your vibration is high. This leads to you becoming more magnetic to people, success and opportunities. You have a positive expectation that good things will come your way and usually they do.

You place a greater value on yourself, which means that you value your time, as well as your products and services. This enables you to communicate with people to create new projects in such a way that is beneficial to all, including you. Other people then start to value you, which means that they are more likely to pay you what you are really worth. So money can flow much easier to you in ever increasing amounts.

### Living Life on the Spiral

As a woman with everything connected, you experience your days on a spiral. On a bad day you spiral downwards and on good day you spiral upwards. If you start at neutral, it does not take very much for your whole day to move on the spiral, up or down, positively or negatively. The further away you get from the neutral position, the more the emotions are magnified.

This seems to be especially true of negative spiralling. My experience has been that it takes less than five minutes to go from a "bad hair day" to a day that is a "disaster of epic proportions" and it can be very difficult to turn that around.

The key is to introduce pleasure when you are in a neutral place or already on your upward spiral and then push it upwards as fast as you can. Think of an aeroplane taking off. It expends a lot of energy to get off the ground, but it does so quickly. Once it is at cruising altitude, it is easier to maintain that place with far less energy, and the aeroplane can almost fly itself! You have got to overcome the inertia of starting.

If you find yourself going down a negative spiral, it is important to catch this as soon as possible and change it around, so you are back on the upward pleasure path. In chapter six, I give you some quick techniques that you can use to get your energies back on the upward track and stimulate your orgasm energy.

The good news is you can inject pleasure into your life very quickly and turn everything around.

## The Spiral Diagram

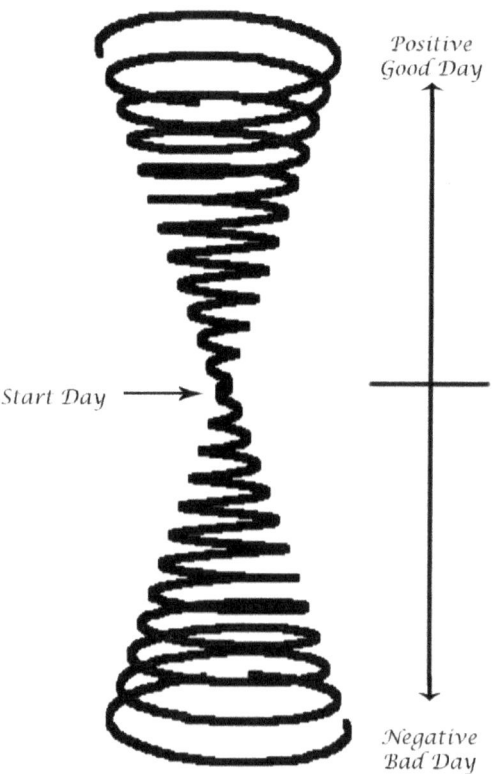

Let's have a look at both types of day.

## Negative Downward Spiral Day

The fact that everything is connected to everything else is usually portrayed as being very negative and a great disadvantage to a woman. As an example, you might have gone to put on your favourite pair of trousers and thought they felt a bit tight. This can then lead into you thinking you have put on weight, deciding that you are fat and that you really don't like yourself very much.

Women can be very unkind to themselves. This might lead to you then trying to find something else to wear, and discover that everything in your wardrobe is either not suitable, has holes in it or needs ironing, so you wear what you were originally going to wear, but rush out the door stressed and late. You have just started on a negative downward spiral.

Should something unexpected happen like your car breaks down and, whilst you are at work, you get a phone call advising you that the repair bill is three times what you thought it was going to be. That can push you further down the negative spiral, especially if you had not budgeted for that much money. It might be that you start to think that paying the repair bill has now ruined your chances of having a holiday, as it is going to take the money that you had allocated to paying for your holiday.

That phone call then impacts your ability to make a rational decision about an important business matter. You are then worrying about the car repair bill, which causes you to snap at people around you, who then make mistakes because they have not clearly understood what you wanted them to do, so you end up doing everything yourself and forgetting to make an important phone call, which could have led to new business.

When you finally get home, you open the door, fall over the post on the doormat, break a heel on your shoe and sink into a frazzled heap in a chair. By now, your stress levels have gone through the roof, so you reach for a glass of wine and a bar of chocolate for comfort. These give you a momentary high and then you beat yourself up for ruining your diet. You certainly don't feel like going to that evening's exercise class, although you know it would probably do you good to go!

So everything is connected to everything else and your day just went from bad to worse.

**Growth Through Pain is Past History**

If you have tried creating growth and change in your life, then chances are that has been quite a painful process. It has probably involved a lot of introspection and looking at what is not working for you and why it has not worked.

I have done this for years, and I have not found it to be particularly effective. This is because you end up focusing on the pain and that does not clear it. I have found that, after doing these type of processes, I would end up in a place of "What's wrong with me?" and "Why can't I make my life work?"

Not very helpful!

Actually looking at all this stuff can quickly start you off on a negative, downward spiral, as discussed in the example above.

**Break the Pain Cycle with Pleasure**

If you are fed up with trying to create transformation in your life through difficulty, pain and challenge and you are looking for a way that is easier and much more fun, then I have a solution for you.

Break the pain cycle through the introduction of pleasure and watch what happens. For this to be really effective, it needs to be something that you actually feel in your body, not just something that you think about.

**Drum Roll, Please!**

*Orgasm!*

One of the most enjoyable ways to introduce pleasure into your body is through an orgasm, thus stimulating the pleasure sensors,, not the pain sensors, in your body and brain.

### Orgasmic Pleasuring

This is a fabulous way to break the negative cycle. It changed my whole outlook on life and it is one of the most pleasurable ways to experience transformation that I have ever come across.

If you can allow yourself to relax enough to receive the gift of an OP (Orgasmic Pleasuring) session, it can help to stabilise you and your emotions very quickly. There is no goal with the practice, so it does not matter whether you have an orgasm or not. Just lie back and enjoy.

### So, Why do Orgasms Break a Negative Cycle?

The Laws of Physics tell us that things – and people as well – will essentially keep moving in the same direction, either positive or negative, unless they are acted upon by an external stimulus. This might mean that something happens to you and you react to it in a particular way, which changes how you think, feel and act for the rest of the day. Likewise you can change something yourself, which can be as simple as deciding to think a different thought, feel differently about something or take a different action.

So, essentially this means that if everything stays the same for you, then your results in any area will be the same.

Let's go back to our example above and see how that same situation could create an upward spiral of pleasure.

### An Upward Spiral of Pleasure Day

You have had the pleasure of a wonderful orgasm, either the previous night or - better still – that morning. You look in the mirror and see your glowing "pleasured woman" look and say "Good Morning, Gorgeous!" to the beautiful face looking back at you.

If your trousers are tight, then perhaps that is a good thing because you have been doing a lot of expanding and contracting of your abdomen muscles during Orgasm, so it is probably stomach muscles developing (YAY!). You might wear your trousers or you might just decide to opt for your lovely flirty skirt because you feel really good in that – and it shows off your legs.

In this place, everything is likely to flow for you, from traffic lights being on green as you approach, to someone holding the door open for you as you get to the office. If you travel by public transport, you might strike up a conversation with someone that opens up new business possibilities for you.

When you get the phone call about your car repair bill, you are more likely to see if you can negotiate on the price or whether you can come to a payment arrangement with the garage. Yes, the bill is more than you thought, but your holiday is important because you have been working very hard and deserve a break. In dealing with the car repair bill, you might also sit down with a piece of paper and ask yourself how you can generate the extra money you need, so that your approach becomes "BOTH AND", rather than "EITHER OR."

Still being in a positive place, you can clearly and confidently communicate with your team, so they know what you want them to do and this gives you the time to prepare for that important phone call. This means that you know exactly what you want to accomplish and how to gain a win-win for everyone.

When you get home, you are still buzzing from the positive events of the day, so you are quite likely to pick up your sports bag and go to the exercise class, and then nourish your body with healthy food. At the end of the day, with your mind still focused on fun, you will probably find other activities to do that bring you even more pleasure. Maybe more orgasms!

## CHAPTER TWELVE – PLEASURE RULES OK!

### Your Pleasure Declaration

Set YOUR PLEASURE DECLARATION that you are going to allow yourself to experience orgasms on a regular basis and that you will make you and your pleasure the number ONE priority in your life.

When you do that, everything flows.

Use the power of "It's All Connected!" to live a pleasure filled life that is an upward spiral of energy and fun.

A daily Orgasm can transform your life and the lives of people around you.

Keep Practising!


### I am championing a Pleasure Revolution!

Come and join me in changing the lives and prosperity of women across the globe by making pleasure your number one priority – and enjoy some jolly good orgasms along the way!

## Testimonials

Amanda Goldston has written an engaging, easy to read book that has something for all women.  She has certainly opened my eyes to the energetic benefits of orgasms, and I since reading her book, I find I have a far more playful attitude to including orgasmic energy in my life.

Sue M  Coventry.

_____

In this book Amanda shares how she harnessed her feminine energies to spiral her personal success and prosperity upwards - and how you can do the same. You may need an open mind to explore her 'orgasmic' instruction but as you read the book you will sense her 'wicked' sense of humour and almost hear her 'raucous cackle'.  If you are new to energy this book will help you understand the main energy centres of the body and how they correspond to colour and your personal power. Amanda's messages are simple - value yourself more, let go of guilt, be more open to receive and say yes to things you truly desire.   Everything is the energy of pleasure - treat yourself like the Queen that you are!

Liz Keaney - Speaker and Author '*Warrior Women – How to be Magnificent through the Courage of Self Kindness*'.   www.lizkeaney.com

## References and Bibliography

Orgasm Your Way to Prosperity, Amanda Goldston, Goldston Group, Tamworth, 2015

Emergence of the Sensual Woman, Saida Desilets, PhD, Jade Goddess Publishing, Maui, 2006

Healing Simplified, Tonya Cox Turrell and Carolanne Anselmo, Healing Energy and Learning 2015

Mama Gena's School Of Womanly Arts: Using The Power Of Pleasure To Have Your Way With The World: How To Use The Power Of Pleasure – Regena Thomashauer – Simon & Shuster, New York 2002

Slow Sex: The Art And Craft Of The Female Orgasm By Daedone, Nicole, Grand Central Life And Style, New York – 2012

Think and Grow Rich by Napoleon Hill, The Ralston Society 1937

## ABOUT THE AUTHOR – AMANDA GOLDSTON

I graduated from The University of Salford in 1989 with a BA (Hons) in Modern Languages. Whilst at University I started in a telesales position to fund myself. Sales seemed a natural choice of career.

I worked in various positions as a self-employed sales person in industries as diverse as encyclopaedias, driveways, booklet advertising and ended up as one of the top sales reps in a national window and conservatory company where I worked for 6 ½ years. I went back to this industry in 2013 and sold over £600,000 of business in a 12 month period.

From my early 20s I have read and studied widely in the fields of personal development, sales and using the mind to create success.

I have also worked with tarot cards to identify limiting beliefs to success and then used a variety of techniques, including energy healing to clear them.

I created my first two audio relaxations in 2003. These were "Clear Limiting Beliefs" and "Creative Problem Solver" which have been transforming lives ever since.

## My Journey with Orgasm Energy

I was in a high-pressure job and was reasonably successful, but I noticed that it was having a detrimental effect on my marriage.

In February 2014 I was listening to a series of interviews about women stepping into their personal power by really tapping into the uniquely female energies in their bodies and harnessing them to create success in their lives.

I started to make PLEASURE a PRIORITY in every area of my life, including the immense amounts of pleasure my physical body could give me, in the form of Orgasms and Orgasmic Energy.

From there, I started to notice, that when I was able to harness these powerful energies in my body, my sales went up and so did my income. Actually, the number of sales did not really increase, but I found I was earning more money from each individual sale, working less hours and covering fewer appointments. I was feeling so much better and so much more alive and that was obviously reflected in my energy and everything about me

As I continued to increase my orgasm energy and to make me and my pleasure a priority, I found that certain things began to fall away. There were situations and people that I was no longer prepared to tolerate in my life because they did not nourish me. I realised that I did not feel valued in my job. I was often working more than 60 hours per week over 6 days, so I was exhausted. My boss would kick up a huge fuss when I tried to book any days off. He frequently told me that my family was not important and that the only ingredient for success was non-stop work.

There were constant battles over money, which were incredibly draining and demotivating.

I needed to earn money to fund my daughters through University, so I kept going for as long as I could. I gradually came to realise that I really did not like this job and I did not want to do it.

When I started to increase my orgasm pleasure, I wrote out some little cards that I kept in my car and my diary that said, "How can I enjoy even more pleasure in my life and my work today?" The more I looked at these cards, the more I realised that I was not valuing myself in my job and was putting up with things that did not support me.

As my energy raised, I finally came to the conclusion that me and the job were completely incompatible. I could not see the company changing, so the only option was for me to honour myself and to move on.

I have to say, I am immensely grateful to that company for giving me a good income during that time. This enabled us to do some fantastic things that really took us upwards on the positive spiral.

I am based in the Midlands, UK.

I am happily married to my friend and soulmate, Greg, my partner of nearly 30 years and we have two wonderful daughters.

## OTHER RESOURCES

www.thepleasurepathtowealth.com

I have a range of transformational audio relaxation products and other products, which are designed to help you to create Pleasure and ease in your life, in bite-sized pieces.

### Orgasm Your Way to Prosperity – 8 Day Video Course

This short course expands on the ideas and practices in this book.

http://amandagoldston.com/thepleasurepathtowealth/index.php/orgasm-your-way-to-prosperity-8-day-video-course-uk/

There are lots of articles and resources in the MAD Woman Academy section on my website.

## Tarot Author and Teacher

I am also a Tarot Author and Teacher and show people how to use Tarot Cards for personal growth, understanding the people around them and for creative problem solving.

When you combine your orgasm energies with a card reading, you can get tremendous insights and amazing information.

I am the author of 3 tarot books, which you can find on amazon kindle and on my website – http://www.learntarotonline.com

There is a free tarot card of the Day Reading and I send out Weekly Tarot Tips to help you to learn to get the best answers from your tarot cards.

## CONTACT

http://www.AmandaGoldston.com

Email: info@amandagoldston.com

Tel: +44 (0) 1827 52995

My Twitter Page - @Amanda_Goldston

My LinkedIn Profile - https://www.linkedin.com/in/amandagoldston/

www.ingramcontent.com/pod-product-compliance
Lightning Source LLC
Chambersburg PA
CBHW070456090426
42735CB00012B/2577